RAINY DAY ACTIVITIES

TOP THAT™

Licensed exclusively to Top That Publishing Ltd
Tide Mill Way, Woodbridge, Suffolk, IP12 1AP, UK
www.topthatpublishing.com
Copyright © 2017 Tide Mill Media

Tumbling Butterfly

You will need:

- Square sheet of paper
- Coloring pens or pencils to decorate the Tumbling Butterfly

This acrobatic flier gracefully tumbles as it flies through the air. Make your flier look extra special by decorating it with a design like the one shown above, or create your own design.

Fold the square sheet of paper in half from right to left, as shown.

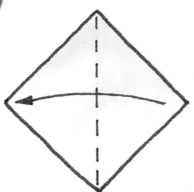

Fold and unfold in half from bottom to top. (This is called a valley fold.)

Fold the left-hand point over so that it overlaps the right-hand side.

4 Now fold in half from bottom to top.

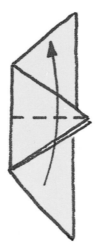

5 Fold the front flap forward and the back flap behind, making the Tumbling Butterfly's wings.

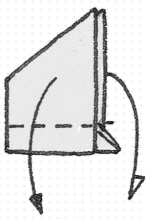

6 Lift the wings up so that they are horizontal. Open them out a little, as shown. This completes the Tumbling Butterfly.

7 Hold the Tumbling Butterfly between thumb and forefinger. Throw it forward with a slight push up. As it falls, it will gracefully tumble over and over.

Balloon Jet

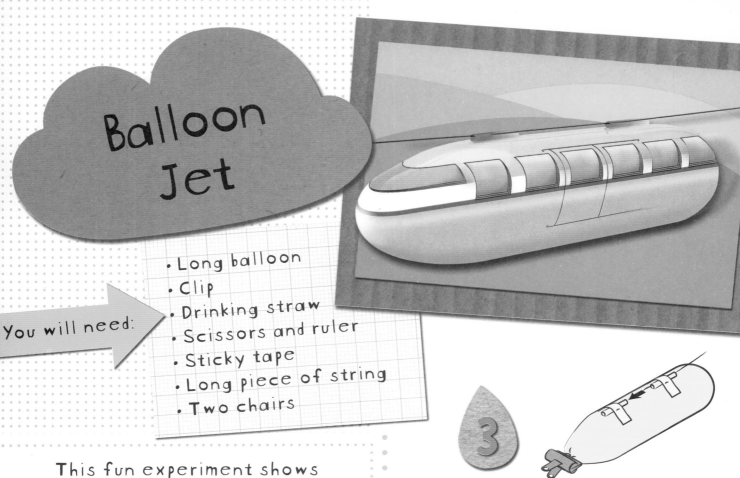

You will need:

- Long balloon
- Clip
- Drinking straw
- Scissors and ruler
- Sticky tape
- Long piece of string
- Two chairs

This fun experiment shows how a simple balloon can be transformed into a rocket using jet propulsion.

1 Inflate the balloon as far as it will go—if you have a balloon pump to hand, you will find it is easier than blowing! Seal the end with the clip.

2 Cut two 2 in. lengths of drinking straw and tape them in a straight line to the top of the balloon, one at each end.

3 Tie one end of the piece of string to one of the chairs. Thread the other end through the pieces of straw, then tie it to the other chair. Move the chairs so the string is stretched tight. Decorate the balloon to look like a jet.

4 Slide the clip end of the balloon toward one of the chairs.

5 Remove the clip, and the balloon will shoot along the string!

Jet-propelled Bottle Car

You will need:

- Thick card
- Scissors and ruler
- Sticky putty
- Two pencils
- Small, empty plastic bottle
- Sticky tape
- Vinegar
- Tissue
- Water
- Baking soda
- Cork

In this experiment, vinegar and water react with baking soda to create gas. This builds up, until the pressure in the bottle makes the cork fly out, propelling the bottle in the opposite direction.

1 Cut four circles from the card, each one 2 in. in diameter. Make a hole in each circle by placing them one at a time on top of the sticky putty and pushing the sharpened end of a pencil through the center. Put one wheel on each end of the pencils to make two axles.

2 Stick the axles to the bottom of the bottle with sticky tape, as shown.

3 Put one half cup each of water and vinegar into the bottle. Put one heaped teaspoon of baking soda in the middle of the tissue, pulling up the edges of the tissue and twisting the top so the baking soda cannot escape.

4 Take your prepared bottle outside. Drop the tissue and baking soda into the bottle, and push the cork into the top. Place the bottle on its wheels, then stand back and wait.

5 Gradually, the gas will build up inside the bottle and the cork will shoot off, propelling the bottle forward.

Printing Letters

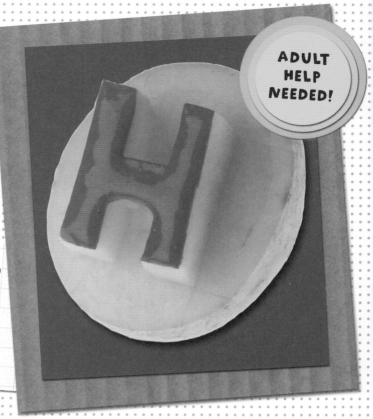

You will need:

- Medium-sized potato
- Knife
- Kitchen roll
- Poster paint
- Card or paper

Here's a simple printing technique which you can do using potatoes. Use different-sized potatoes and a selection of colors to achieve a wide variety of effects. Cutting out a letter "H" to print is easy, but other letters are a bit more tricky—remember, always cut your letters out back to front so that they print the right way round.

 Cut the top off the potato.

 Now cut off the edges of the potato halfway down, so that you are left with a rectangular block.

 Cut a letter from the rectangular block.

 Dry the top of the letter with kitchen roll, then dip it face down into the paint. Make sure it has a good, even coating.

 Gently press your potato letter onto the card, then lift it off to reveal your printed letter.

Pretty Popsicles

You will need:

- ½ cup lemon or pineapple drink
- ½ cup orange juice
- Jug
- Popsicle molds

There will be bursts of delicious flavors in these citrus popsicles!

1 Pour the first flavored drink into the popsicle molds, along with a splash of water, until each mold is about half full. Place the molds into the freezer and leave them to set for at least **4 hours**, until solid.

2 Repeat the process, but this time with the different—flavored juice. Pour on top of the frozen layer and place into the freezer, until solid.

3 Remove the posicless from the molds and enjoy!

Erupting Volcano

- Modeling clay (for example, green, brown, gray and orange colored)
- A baking tray
- 1 tablespoon baking soda
- Tiny scrunched up paper balls
- Vinegar

ADULT HELP NEEDED!

Volcanoes are amazing natural spectacles. However, while they look awesome, the danger that an erupting volcano presents to us is a reminder that we have little power over the natural world. Construct your own volcano with modeling clay, then make your own volcanic eruption.

Make your own volcano

1 Use any color of modeling clay you want to build the shape of a volcano, leaving a shallow recess in the center.

2 Add layers of modeling clay to provide your volcano with colors and textures. You could put green at the bottom to represent grass and trees, then brown, orange and gray above to represent mud and grass. You could even add real grass from your backyard for an authentic volcano look.

Volcanic eruption

 1 Put your volcano on a baking tray because this experiment is messy!

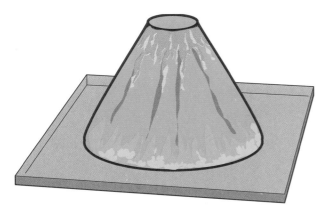

2 Pour a tablespoon of baking soda into the crater with the tiny scrunched up paper balls.

 **3** Mix the powder and the tiny scrunched up paper balls until they lie flat in the crater.

4 Spoon a small amount of the vinegar into the crater. Stand back and watch the eruption!

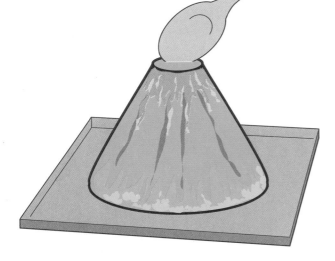

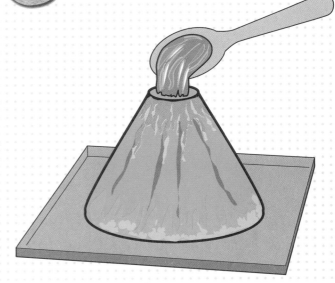

The vinegar reacts with the baking soda to make carbon dioxide. As in real volcanoes, carbon dioxide gas bubbles escape at the surface into the atmosphere. The paper balls represent larger rocks that are blasted out of some volcanoes.

Balloon Mouse

Some very small bubbles make up this little balloon character. You will need to squeeze the air out of some of them before you twist, so that they are only half as fat as the main balloon.

2 Squeeze and twist a 1½ in. bubble and then twist it to the head.

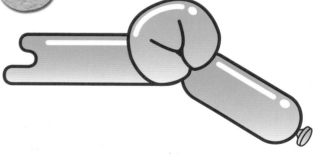

1 Begin with a long balloon inflated to just 8 in. Squeeze and twist a 2 in. bubble for the head.

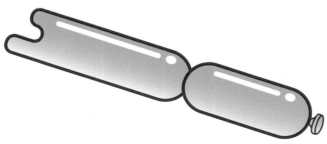

3 Squeeze and twist another 1½ in. bubble. Then twist it next to the first.

Hold the balloon knot and tug it down and around to make the head bubble curve and look more mouse-like.

4 Squeeze and twist a ¾ in. bubble for the neck and two more ¾ in. bubbles for the front legs.

Bend and twist the legs together next to the neck.

5 Squeeze and twist a 1½ in. bubble for the body and two ¾ in. bubbles for the back legs.

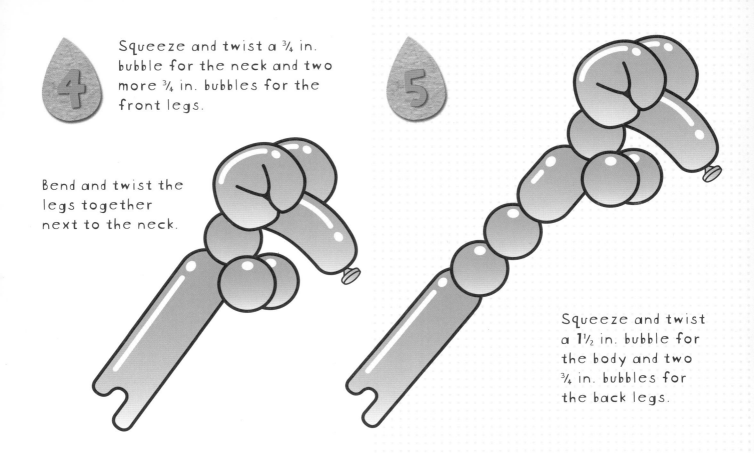

6 Twist the back legs together behind the body.

7 You should have a small bubble (about ¾ in.) and a long piece of balloon left over to be the mouse's tail. Finish your mouse with eyes, nose and whiskers drawn in black marker pen.

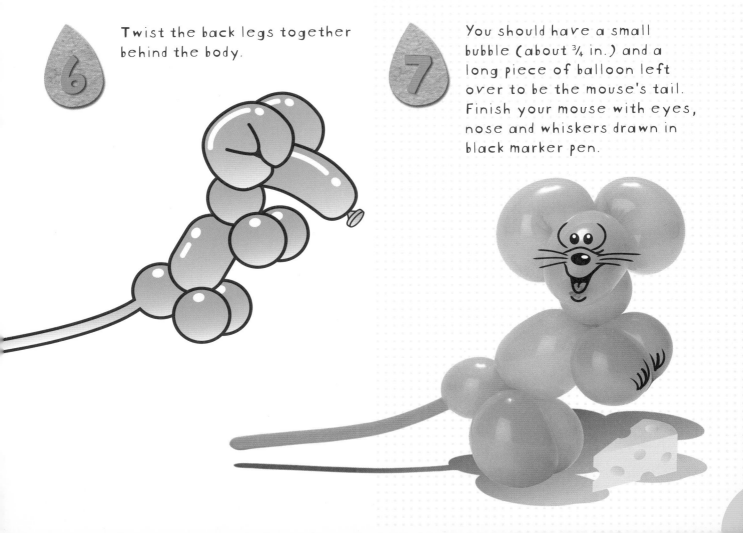

Cheesy Straws

You will need:

- **1** stick of butter
- **⅔** cup of shredded cheese
- **1** cup all-purpose flour
- **1** free-range egg yolk
- Baking tray
- Baking parchment
- Grater
- Large bowl
- Sieve
- Rolling pin
- Knife
- Cooling rack

Quick and easy to make, these delicious cheesy straws are best eaten while they are still warm from the oven!

 Preheat the oven to 400°F. Grease a baking tray with a little butter and cover it with a piece of baking parchment.

 Shred the cheese.

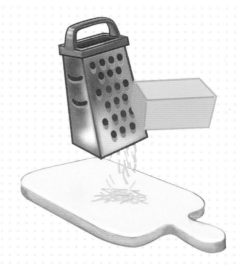

Place the cheese into a bowl and sift in the flour with a sieve.

Cut the butter into small cubes and rub them into the mixture with your fingers.

When the mixture is crumbly and the butter has almost disappeared, stir in the egg yolk.

Next, roll the pastry into a ball. Then, dust the work surface with plenty of flour and roll out the pastry into a rough square approximately ¼ in. thick.

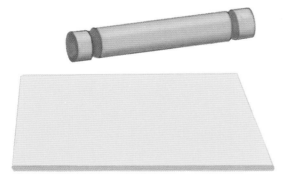

Cut the square into strips and transfer them onto the baking sheet. Ensure that you leave a small space between each one.

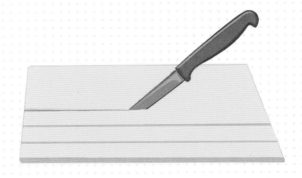

Ask an adult to place the baking parchment into a preheated oven and bake for about 7 minutes or until the cheesy straws are a pale golden brown. Transfer the cheesy straws to a cooling rack and allow to cool. Yum, yum!

Periscope

You will need:

- A long, thin box
- Scissors
- Mirror board
- Craft knife
- Sticky tape
- Green and brown paint (optional)

ADULT HELP NEEDED!

With its clever arrangement of mirrors, this periscope will help you see objects that are out of your line of sight—perfect for peeking around corners or over walls!

Ask an adult to help you cut two diagonal slits at the top of the box. These should be on opposite sides.

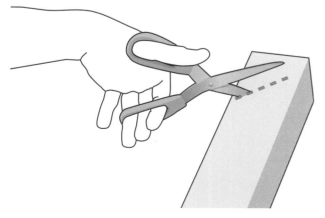

Connect these slits by cutting a third slit straight across the front.

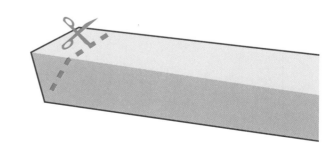

Ask an adult to cut two pieces of mirror board that are the same area as the box top area. Then slide a mirror into the top of the box.

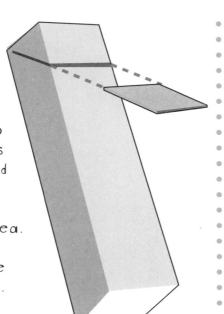

Fix the mirror in place with sticky tape.

Cut identical slits, following steps 1–2, at the bottom of the box. Make sure you cut the opposite side of the box.

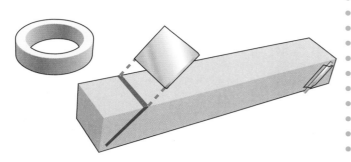

Fix the second mirror into the space as before using sticky tape.

Cut a square in the side of the box facing each mirror. Your periscope is now ready to use. For super spying, paint your periscope in camouflage colors to avoid detection!

Invincible String

You will need:
- A long piece of string
- Scissors
- A drinking straw

Cut a piece of string but keep it in one piece—or so it seems!

1

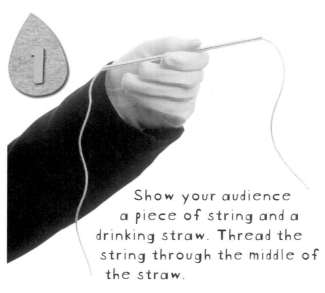

Show your audience a piece of string and a drinking straw. Thread the string through the middle of the straw.

2

Bend the straw in half and cut right through the center.

3 Now remove the string—still in one piece!

But how?

Before your show, cut a short slit along the center of the straw. When you bend the straw in half to cut it, pull the ends of the string. This will pull it through the slit in the straw. Keep this covered with your hand, and the string is not touched at all when you cut!

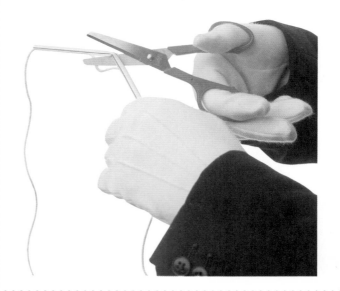

Magnetic Sculpture

You will need:

- Small cardboard box
- Sticky tape
- Round magnet
- Small steel items, such as pins, paper clips, nails and screws

With a few carefully placed paper clips and nails you can use magnetism to create your own modern art sculpture!

1 Tape a magnet to the inside of the cardboard box, then flip the box over.

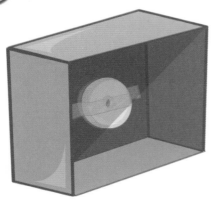

2 Place some of the small steel items—like the paper clips—onto the box, above the magnet.

3 Add other metallic objects to the box and shape them into a sculpture.

It may not be pretty, but it's still art!

Cargo Plane

You will need:

- Two large, square water bottles
- Scissors, ruler and pencil
- One small yogurt pot
- Strong school glue
- Thick card
- Four identical small soda bottles
- One thin cardboard kitchen roll tube
- Paint and paintbrushes
- White and colored paper
- A black marker pen
- Four clear round plastic lids
- Thin white card

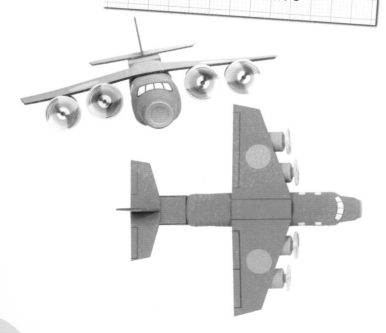

The main construction materials for this large cargo plane are two empty plastic water bottles and some cardboard. The model includes some clever details, such as the engines made from small soda bottles and propellers created from plastic lids.

Take your time painting the authentic colors and adding more details to the bodywork with a black marker pen, so your plane looks like the real thing!

18

Building a cargo plane

 **1** Find two large water bottles that are square in shape. Cut the top off one of them and the bottom off the other one, as shown.

2 Using scissors, make a cut approx 1 in. long at each corner of the bottle with the bottom removed. Now carefully cut the neck off the bottle, as shown. Push this bottle onto the other one, as shown, until you get a firm fit.

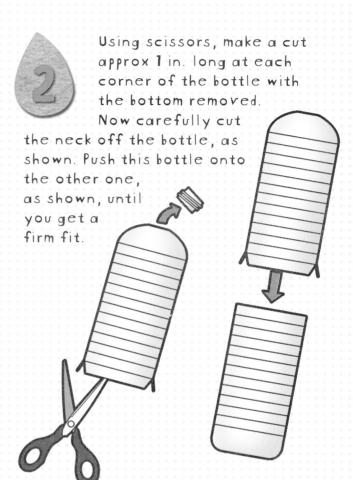

3 Take a small yogurt pot and ask for adult assistance to neatly cut ½ in. off the top so that you get rid of its lip. Use glue to fix the yogurt pot to the bottles from step 2, as shown.

4 Copy the wing template provided (see page 23) onto a sheet of thick card twice and cut the shapes out. Glue the two wing shapes together, then glue onto the middle of the bottles. Leave to dry.

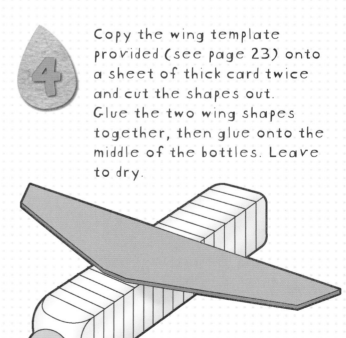

 Copy two small tail templates and one large tail template (see page 23) onto thick card. Cut them all out and then glue together, as shown.

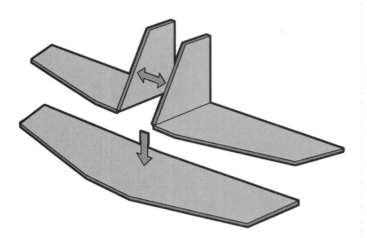

 Copy two of the small rear body template, and one of the large rear body template onto thick card. Cut them all out and then glue them together, as shown.

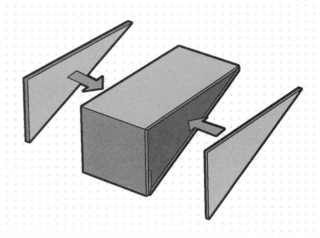

 Glue the tail you made in step 5 onto the rear body you made in step 6. When this is dry, glue the rear body onto the bottom of the bottle structure, as shown.

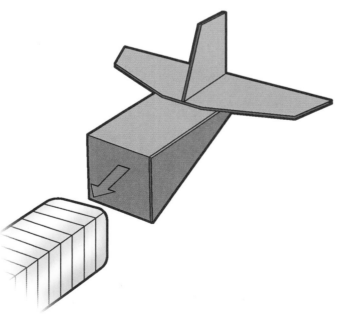

 Find four identical small soda bottles. Lay your plane upside down so that you can see the underneath of the wings. Glue two bottles onto each wing. It is important you make sure that each bottle sticks out over the front of the wings, and that they are evenly spaced, as shown.

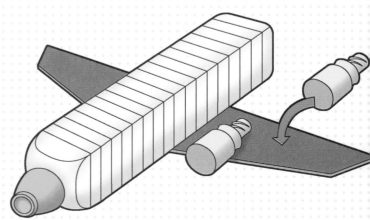

Take a thin cardboard kitchen roll tube and carefully cut four sections from it that are each 1 in. long. Glue one of these sections onto each of the bottles that are attached to the wings, as shown.

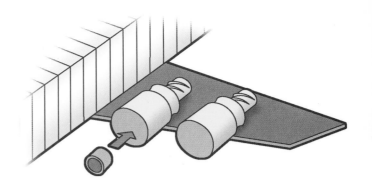

Paint your plane green. Paint the four bottles that are attached to the wings a light gray color to make them look like engines.

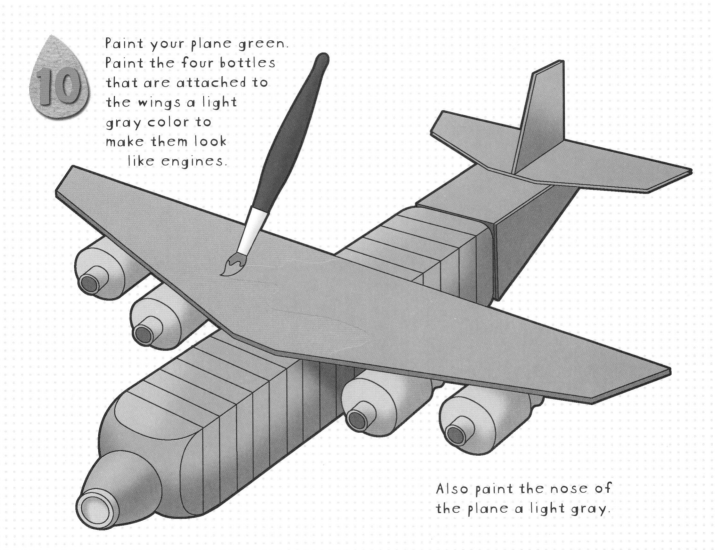

Also paint the nose of the plane a light gray.

Using sheets of white and colored paper, design and glue onto the plane some windows, wing/tail markings and engine panels, as desired.

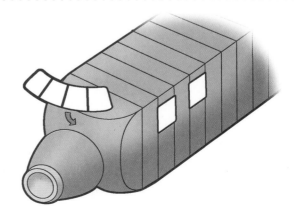

 Take a black marker pen and add panel lines, door hatches, and wing/tail flaps to your plane.

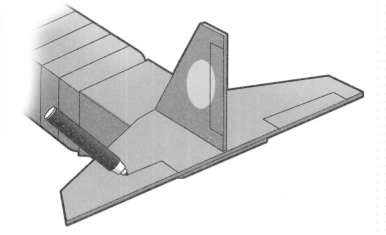

 Find four clear plastic lids, such as those found on round potato chip cartons. With a black marker pen, draw the pattern shown (below) to create the effect of spinning propellers.

Cut four circles from some thin white card. Make these the same diameter as the cardboard kitchen roll tube you used in step 9.

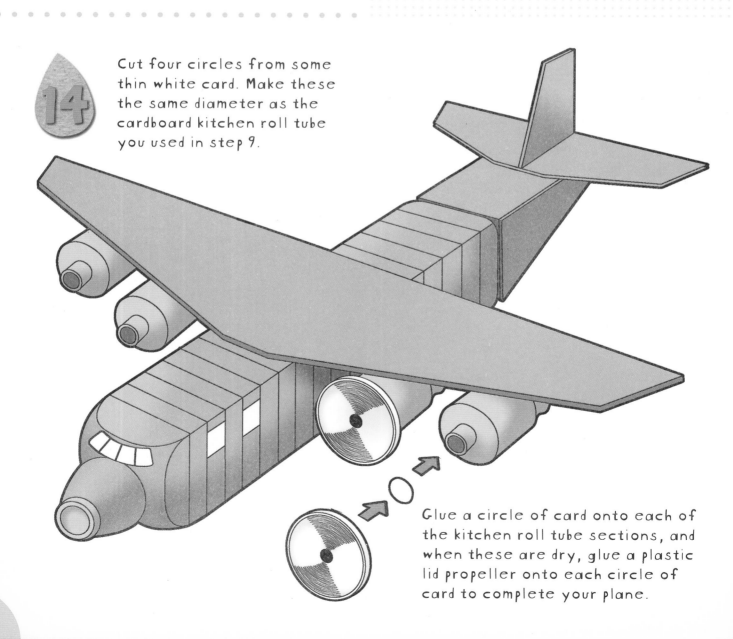

Glue a circle of card onto each of the kitchen roll tube sections, and when these are dry, glue a plastic lid propeller onto each circle of card to complete your plane.

CARGO PLANE TEMPLATES

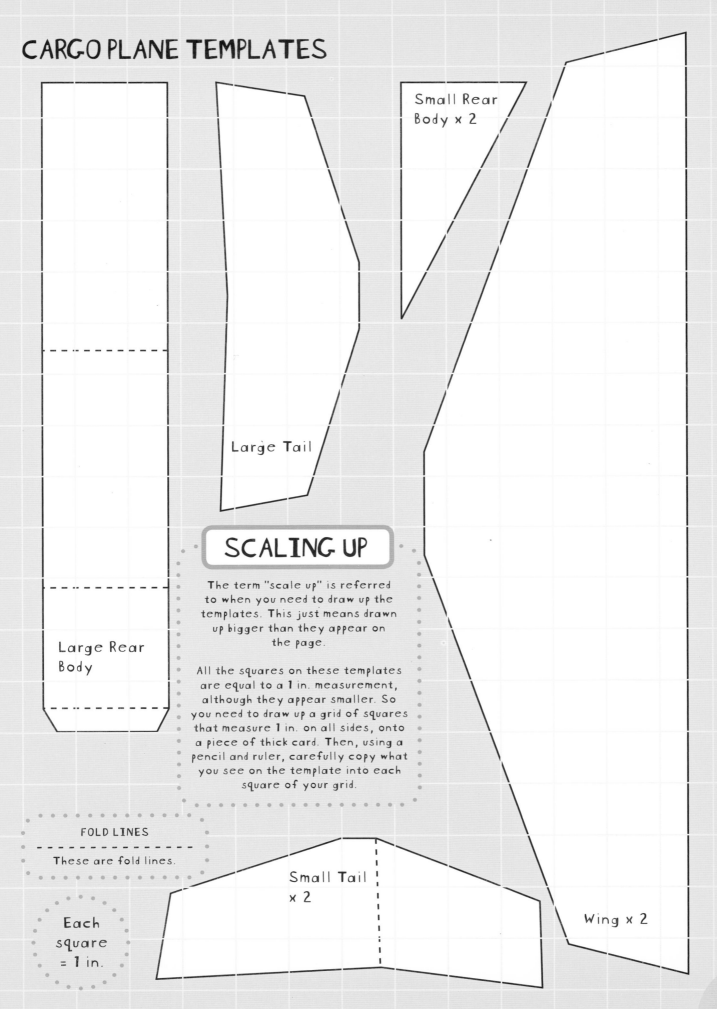

Small Rear
Body x 2

Large Tail

Large Rear
Body

SCALING UP

The term "scale up" is referred to when you need to draw up the templates. This just means drawn up bigger than they appear on the page.

All the squares on these templates are equal to a 1 in. measurement, although they appear smaller. So you need to draw up a grid of squares that measure 1 in. on all sides, onto a piece of thick card. Then, using a pencil and ruler, carefully copy what you see on the template into each square of your grid.

FOLD LINES

- - - - - -

These are fold lines.

Each
square
= 1 in.

Small Tail
x 2

Wing x 2

Sock Puppet

You will need:

- Two table tennis balls
- Paint
- Paintbrushes
- Pencil
- A black marker pen
- Thin white card
- Scissors
- Strong school glue
- A sock

Roar!

Very quick and easy to make, this silly sock puppet will soon have your friends laughing their socks off when you introduce it to them. It's the perfect puppet playpal!

1 Find two table tennis balls. Carefully paint half of each one purple. When these are dry, add pupils and line details to each one with a black marker pen.

2

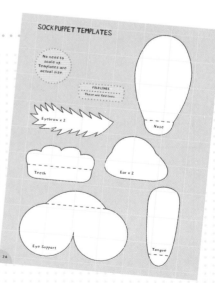

SOCK PUPPET TEMPLATES

Copy the nose, tongue, teeth, ear, eyebrow and eye support templates (see page 26) onto thin white card. (You need two ears and two eyebrows.) Cut these out.

 Paint the ears light pink, the nose and eye support purple, the eyebrows green, the nose pink and purple, and the tongue dark pink. Leave the teeth white. Once all these have dried, draw on details with a black marker pen.

 Glue the eye support, ears and eyebrows to one another. Use the tab on the bottom of the eye support to glue all of the attached items onto the sock, as shown.

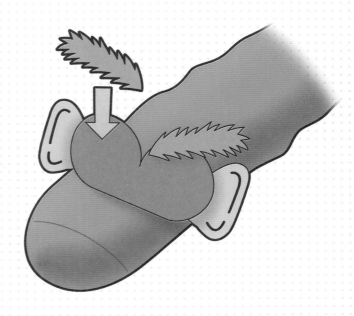

 Glue the table tennis ball eyes from step 1 onto the sock and cardboard eye support, as shown. Hold these in place until the glue dries. Now glue the nose in front of the eyes using its tab.

 Slide the sock onto your hand and form a mouth with it, as shown. Carefully glue the tongue and teeth into this mouth area by using glue on their tabs.

SOCK PUPPET TEMPLATES

No need to scale up. Templates are actual size.

FOLD LINES

These are fold lines.

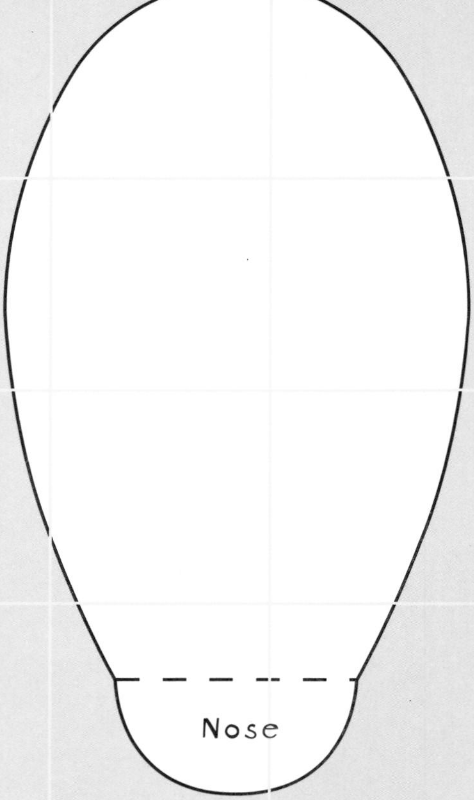

Nose

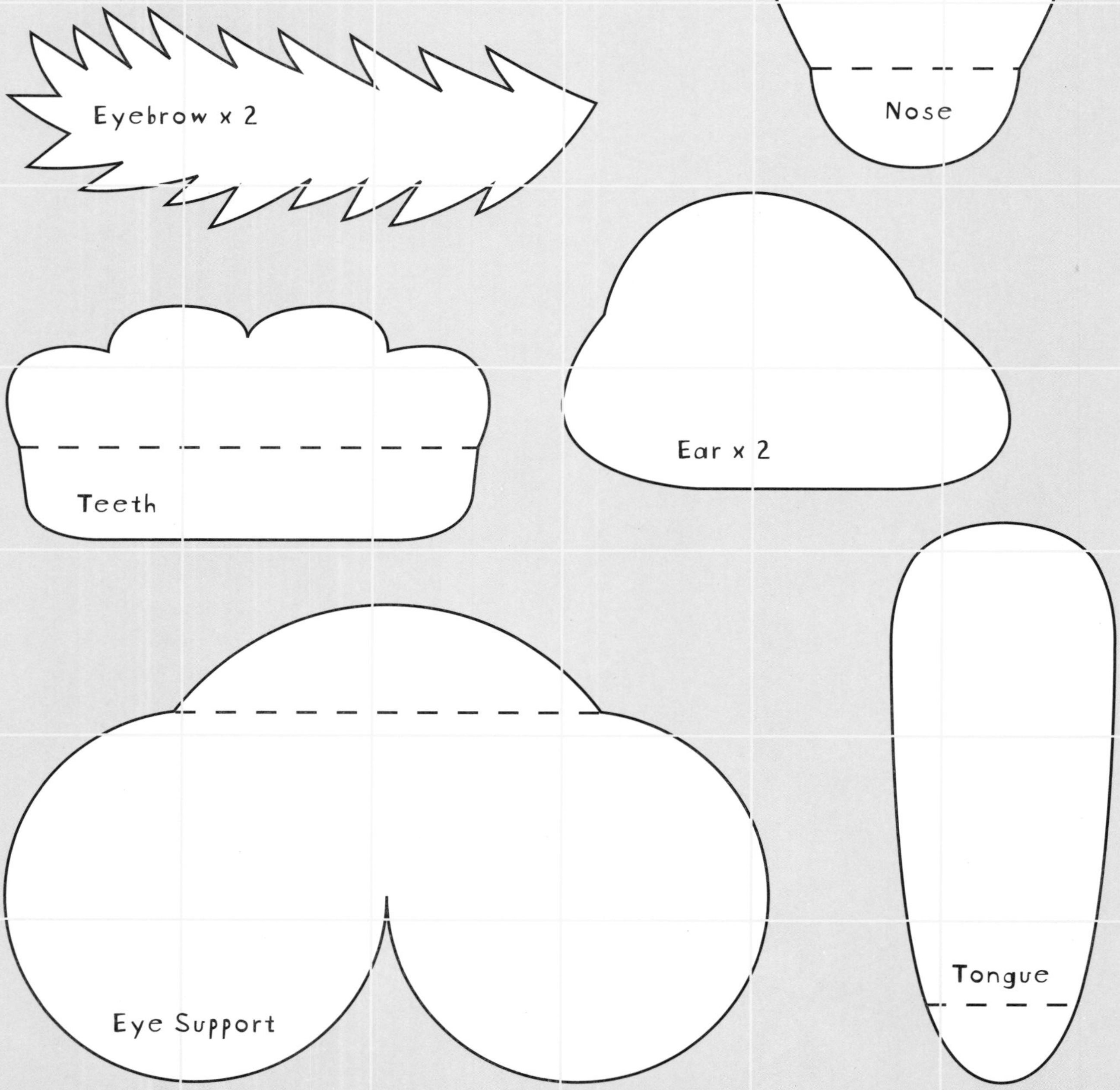

Eyebrow x 2

Ear x 2

Teeth

Tongue

Eye Support

Ice Cream Sundae

You will need:

- ½ cup strawberries, halved
- ¼ cup confectioner's sugar
- ½ tsp. water
- 4 scoops strawberry ice cream
- whipped cream, to decorate
- Glacé cherries, to decorate
- Blender
- Sieve
- Sundae glass
- Piping bag

This delicious fruity sundae is great as an after-school treat!

1 Ask an adult to purée half of the strawberries in a blender with the confectioner's sugar and ½ tsp. of water.

2 Then, carefully push the purée through a sieve to remove the seeds.

3 Pour a small amount of purée into the bottom of a sundae glass, then pile on a scoop of strawberry ice cream and a tablespoon of whipped cream. Repeat the process.

4 Place the remaining whipped cream into a piping bag and pipe it onto the top of the sundae. Top with a whole strawberry or glacé cherry to finish.

Katy Pillar

You will need:

- Three six-egg cartons
- Strong school glue
- Thin card
- Paint
- Paintbrushes
- Pencil and ruler
- A black marker pen
- Colored card (red, yellow and green)
- Scissors

Three egg cartons form the different segments of this caterpillar's body and each of her eighteen feet wears little lace-up shoes! Dotty and spotty patterns look best, so get out your paintbrush and bring Katy the egg carton caterpillar to life.

1 Take three egg cartons and tear off any labels that they have on them. Glue all the lids shut. Glue all three of the cartons together in a line, as shown.

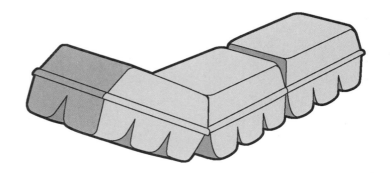

2 Scale up and copy the back template (see page 31) onto a sheet of thin card. Glue this onto the egg cartons, as shown. (This will help to strengthen the egg cartons and hold them together, as well as covering any printing they may have on them.)

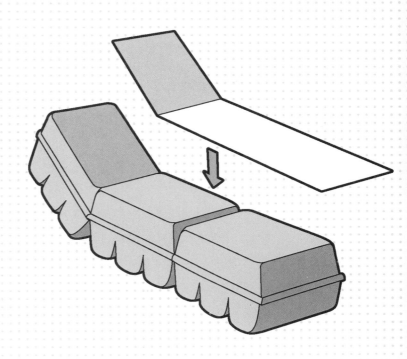

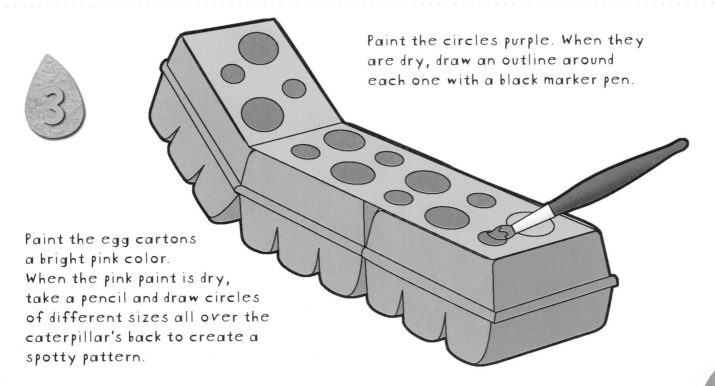

Paint the circles purple. When they are dry, draw an outline around each one with a black marker pen.

3

Paint the egg cartons a bright pink color. When the pink paint is dry, take a pencil and draw circles of different sizes all over the caterpillar's back to create a spotty pattern.

29

 Scale up and copy the foot template provided (see opposite). Draw around this template ten times onto a piece of red card and eight times onto a piece of yellow card. Cut out all the feet and add laces to them using a black marker pen.

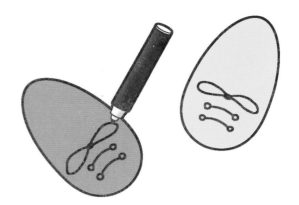

 Using glue, stick the feet to the bottom of the egg cartons. Start at the front of the caterpillar with a pair of red feet, and then alternate between the two colors for each pair, as shown.

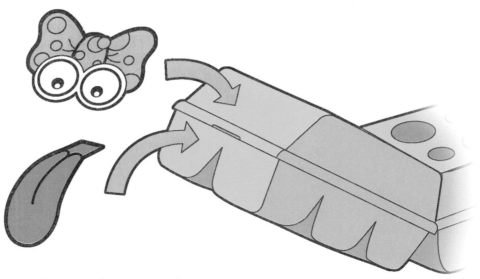

 Scale up and copy the eyes, bow and tongue templates onto colored card. Draw on details with a black marker pen, then glue them in place on the front of your caterpillar to complete the model.

KATY PILLAR TEMPLATES

SCALING UP

The term "scale up" is referred to when you need to draw up the templates. This just means drawn up bigger than they appear on the page.

All the squares on these templates are equal to a 1 in. measurement, although they appear smaller. So you need to draw up a grid of squares that measure 1 in. on all sides, onto a piece of thick card. Then, using a pencil and ruler, carefully copy what you see on the template into each square of your grid.

Each square = 1 in.

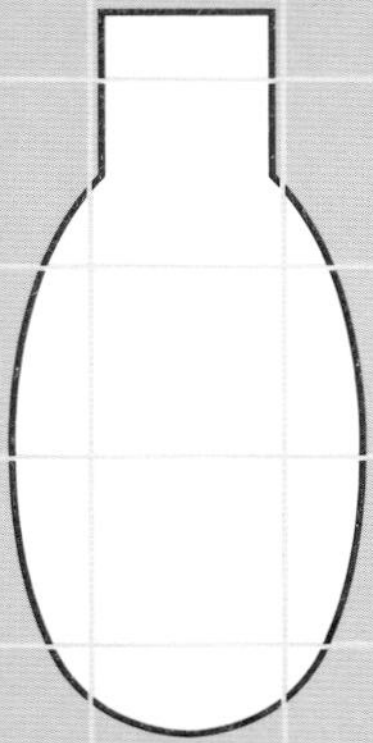

Tongue

Foot x 18

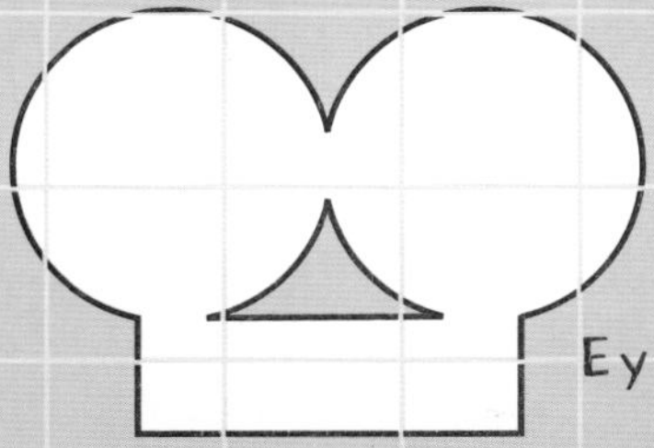

Eyes

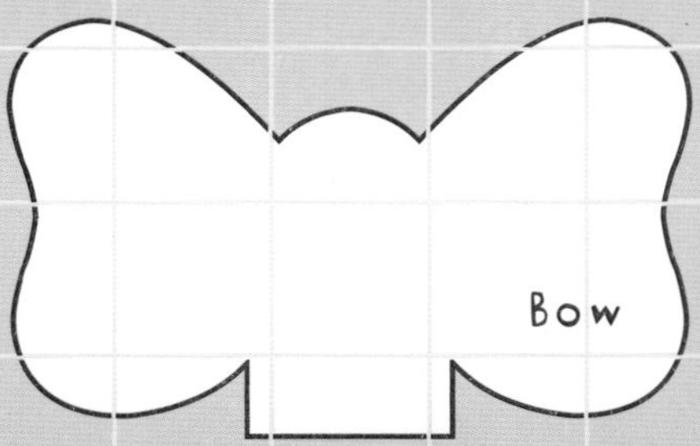

Bow

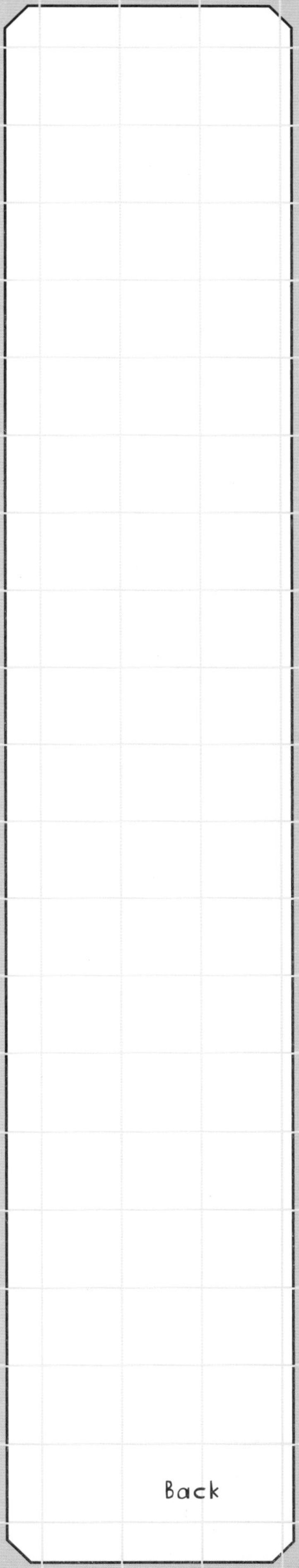

Back

Prank Jokes

Everyone loves to laugh and these practical jokes will have your friends and family in stitches. Before you start, here are a few hints and tips on how to be the world's number one prankster, and ensure that your chosen victim enjoys the prank as well.

1 Never play pranks on a complete stranger as they may not react to the joke in the way that you imagine.

2 Never play pranks on your teacher. Although this may seem like a good idea at the time, an after-school detention is a definite risk!

3 Never play pranks near electrical goods, especially jokes involving water!

4 Always clean up any mess which results from a prank or practical joke.

5 Always be a good sport if someone plays a prank on you.

If you follow these simple rules, there's no limit to the fun you can have.

Fake Puke

You will need:

- Strong school glue
- Yellow paint
- Rice
- Mixing cup
- Colored modeling clay
- Baking Parchment

Make yourself puke—for fun! Not sick, just a great way of grossing out your best friends by making your own pretend puke.

1 Mix the glue, yellow paint and rice together in the mixing cup.

2 Break the modeling clay into little chunks and mix with the rest of the ingredients.

3 Pour the mixture onto some baking parchment to set. When it's dry you will have one portion of instant puke to put where your friends are least expecting it!

Coffee Prank

You will need:
- Brown paint
- Strong school glue
- An old cup
- Baking parchment

If your parents or relatives make you take your shoes off before walking on the carpets, then this practical joke is perfect.

1

Mix some brown paint with some strong school glue.

2

Find the cup you're going to "spill" from, and place it on its side on some baking parchment.

3

Carefully spoon your glue mixture onto the edge of the cup, forming a big pool of pretend drink on the paper. It should look like the mixture is spilling out of the cup.

4

When it's dry, peel it off the parchment and the prank is ready.

5

This "drink" can be spilled anywhere. The more precious the object, the better the reaction!

Avalanche!

u will need:

- Lots and lots of old newspaper
- Sticky tape

There's nothing like opening your curtains on a sunny morning and seeing the birds in the trees and the flowers in the backyard. Then opening your bedroom door and—AVALANCHE!! If there's anyone who you want to cover in snowballs, only there's no snow—now's your chance. You'll need a sleeping dupe to pull this one off.

1 First make sure the door is shut, it opens inward, and your dupe is asleep.

Zzz...
Zzz...
Zzz...

2 Now tape sheets of newspaper across the doorframe, making one big sheet of newspaper, with no gaps, except for a hole at the very top. This is where you're going to fill the space between the door and newspaper sheet with your "snowballs."

3 Screw the newspaper into "snowball" shapes and use them to fill the space. Remember, the more "snowballs" the better the avalanche! Don't make too much noise, you don't want your victim to wake up before the prank is fully operational.

Coin Chuckles

You will need:
- Coin
- Paper
- Pencil

Make sure you do this trick just before the person goes outside so lots of people get to see their new makeup!

 **1** Ask your victim if they're brave enough to take part in a world-famous coordination test.

 2 Ask your victim to place a coin on a piece of paper. Then get them to put their finger on the coin and draw around it with a pencil. Tell them to keep their finger on the coin at all times.

 3 Ask your victim to repeat this exercise using each finger of both hands.

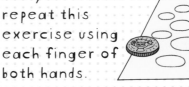

 4 Now comes the devious trickster bit. Tell them that to see if both halves of their brain are coordinated, they have to run the edge of the coin down the center of their face.

5 If they can't do it, then they have failed the test. Of course, everyone can do it, but as you'll see, when they do it they get a big black line down their face! Ha-ha!

Super Prank

ADULT HELP NEEDED!

u will need:
- Needle
- Thread
- Adult permission

If your dad is one of those people who's always in a hurry, then this prank will work even better. Ask your mom or an older sibling to help you with the sewing.

1 Make sure your dad's not around and sneak into his bedroom.

2 Now take two pairs of his underwear and sew them together along one of the edges.

3 Keep sewing the underwear together along the edges to make a big chain.

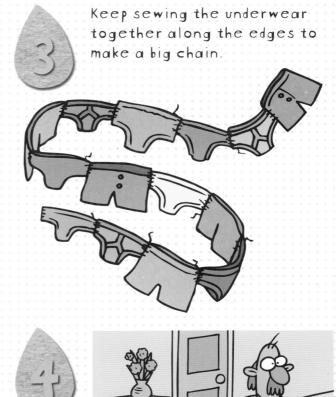

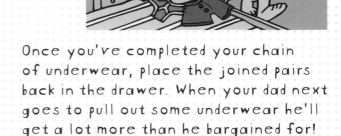

4 Once you've completed your chain of underwear, place the joined pairs back in the drawer. When your dad next goes to pull out some underwear he'll get a lot more than he bargained for!

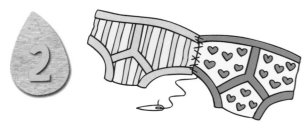

Nice to Snow You

You will need:
- Paper
- Hole punch
- Cardboard box
- Scissors

In the world of the prankster, it doesn't have to be winter for it to snow, at least not on your unsuspecting victim.

 First of all you have to make your snow. Punch lots of holes out of the paper and gather up the hole bits that collect in the bottom.

 Now take your cardboard box and carefully cut a hole in the bottom.

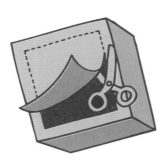

Place the box somewhere your victim will see it—try and put it somewhere above head height and make it look tempting.

Fill the box with the paper snow while it is on the shelf, with the hole resting on the shelf, so none can fall out.

 When your victim spots the box, they'll have to lift it down to see what it is. They'll find themselves covered in fake snow!

Coordination Comedy

Gotcha!

u will need: • Blindfold

This is a prank for all those people who think they know everything, like how fast a walrus can knit and a penguin's favorite flavor of chips (salt and vinegar, obviously).

1 Challenge your victim to take the "blindfold coordination test" and tell them that everyone else has taken it and done really, really well.

2 Sit opposite your victim with your hands about 10 in. apart, palms facing each other. Tell your victim all they have to do is to put their palms together and move their clasped hands between your hands, without making contact.

10 in.

3

Tell them they have to repeat this move as many times as they can, but blindfolded. After letting them have a few practice goes, watching what they're doing, put the blindfold on.

4 Talk them through the first few goes and then, very slowly and quietly, get up and walk away. Your victim will be left sitting there with his hands together, rocking back and forth. Not quite so clever now!

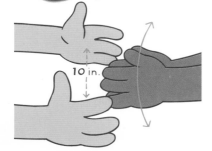

Paper Bird

- A rectangle of colored paper 6¼ in. x 9 in.
- Sticky tape
- Coloring pens

This paper bird has been designed to perform acrobatic loop the loops and a slow graceful flight. Try launching your paper bird from a hilltop or on a windy beach and watch it fly!

1 Using a 6¼ in. x 9 in. rectangle of colored paper, place sideways on and fold and unfold in half from bottom to top.

2 Fold the left-hand corners over to meet the middle fold-line.

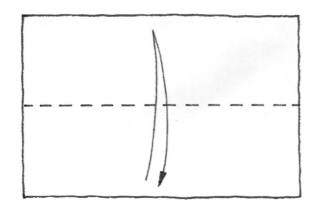

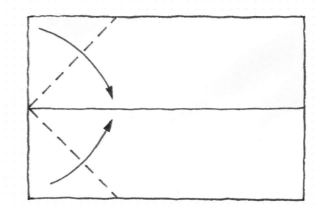

3 Fold the left-hand point over so that it overlaps the right-hand side (see step **4**).

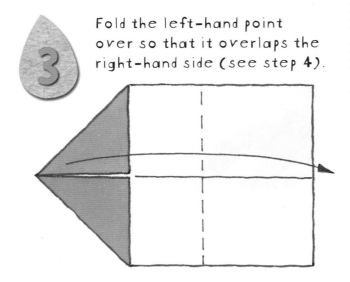

4 Fold the left-hand corners behind to meet the middle fold-line.

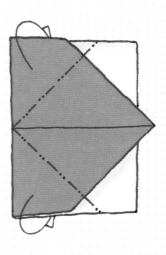

5 Fold the left-hand point over to the right, as shown.

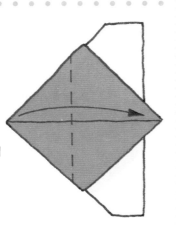

6 Fold the bottom edge behind to meet the top edge.

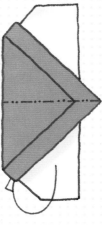

7 Fold the front flap forward and the back flap behind, making the wings.

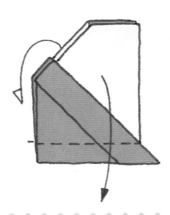

8 Fold over a little of the front wing's bottom edge. Repeat behind.

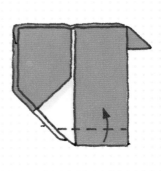

9 Open out the wings, as shown. Hold the wings together with a piece of sticky tape. Now use your coloring pens to add the bird details. To fly, hold the paper bird between your thumb and forefinger and throw it gently forward.

Mosaic Picture Frame

You will need:

- Small photo clip frame 5 in. x 7½ in.
- Paper
- Pencil
- Ruler
- Eraser
- Acrylic paint (pink, yellow, orange, lime green)
- Fine paintbrush

This colorful picture frame will make a great addition to any home!

Lay the clear front of the frame on a piece of paper and draw around it. Make marks at ½ in. intervals along the top, bottom and sides of the rectangle you have drawn. Join the marks with straight lines, from top to bottom and side to side. This will form a grid.

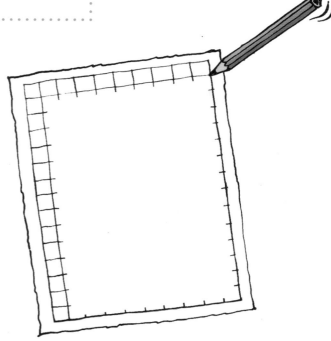

Rub out the center section of the grid, leaving a rectangle large enough to display a photograph. Lay the drawing underneath the glass front once more. This will be the template for your mosaic.

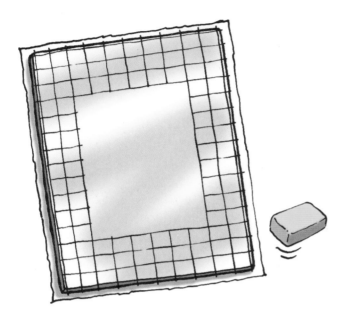

Take one of the colored paints and carefully start to color in the first square on the top row. Do not paint right up to the edge as a tiny border will give the frame a mosaic look when complete. Wash the brush then use a different color to paint the next square. Continue across the frame, changing the color for each square.

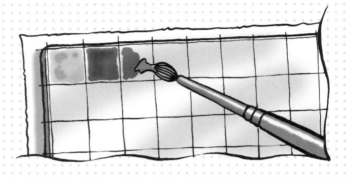

Work on the next row of squares. Make sure that the color you use is different from the square above and next to it. Continue to fill in all of the squares until you reach the bottom of the frame.

Once the paint has dried, turn the glass over and lay it painted side down over your chosen picture. This will stop the paint from being marked when you clip the frame back together.

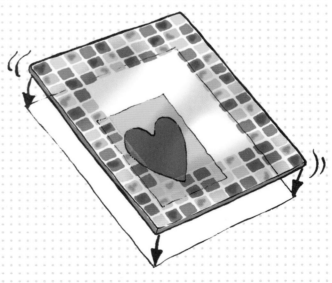

Juggling Skills

You will need:
- 3 juggling balls or cubes

The cascade, or figure eight, is the most common juggling trick you can perform with three objects. This is the first trick most people learn when they start to juggle and will impress your friends.

1

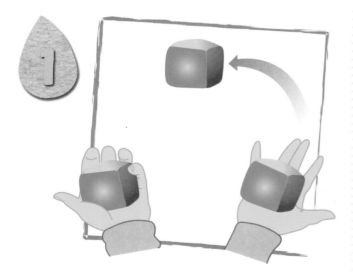

Divide the three cubes so that one is in your left hand and two are in your right hand. Throw one of the cubes in your right hand in an arc. Start counting to keep your timing correct. Count one.

2

When the first cube has reached the top of the arc, throw up the second cube from your left hand. Count to two, by which time you should have caught the first cube in your left hand.

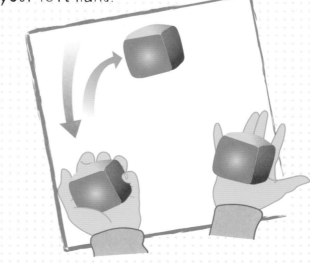

3

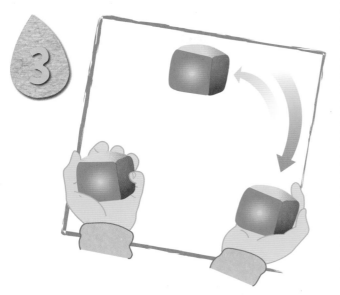

When the second cube reaches the top of the arc, throw up the third cube from your right hand and count to three, by which time you should have caught the second cube in your right hand.

4

When the third cube reaches the top of the arc, throw up the cube from your left hand and count to four. By now, you should have caught the third cube in your left hand.

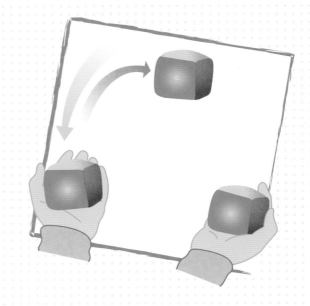

5

When the cube released from your left hand reaches the top of the arc, count to five. Continue in this pattern, throwing the cubes higher each time.

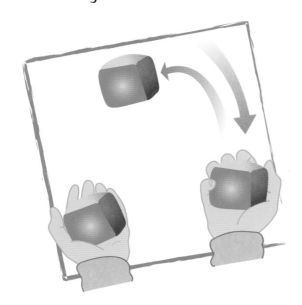

6

Practice, practice, practice! Simply think that each throw is clearing a hand to catch the next cube. Keep the pattern going for as long as possible, and then repeat until you feel really confident.

Papier Mâché Ladybug

ADULT HELP NEEDED!

You will need:

- Newspaper
- Scissors
- Wallpaper glue paste
- Re-sealable container
- Balloon
- Sticky putty
- String
- Tape or strong school glue
- Paints (black, red, white)
- Paintbrush

This cute ladybug model will make a great decoration for your bedroom.

1 Cut lots of strips of newspaper into 1 in. squares. These are used to cover your balloon. Make sure you prepare plenty of strips before you begin because your hands might get a bit sticky.

2 Next, ask an adult to make up 2 cups of wallpaper glue paste.

Mix well and store in a re-sealable container.

3 Blow a balloon up to about 5 in. in length. Dip your fingers into the wallpaper paste and smooth it over the paper until it is slightly soaked (the resulting paper paste mix is called papier mâché). Once the paper is soft it can be easily laid over the balloon. Cover small areas first to check that it sticks on. You can keep the balloon steady with some sticky putty stuck to your work surface.

4

Cover the balloon with 3–4 layers of the glue-covered newspaper.
Tie a piece of string around the knotted end of the balloon and hang it up to dry.

5

To make the legs, scrunch a piece of newspaper into a thin, uneven hot dog shape.

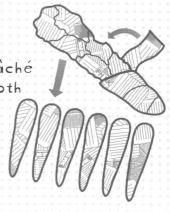

Cover this with a layer of papier mâché to achieve a smooth finish. Repeat until you have made six identical legs. Place these to one side to dry.

6

When all the legs have dried, bind them together with some tape to form a star shape.

Cover the tape with a layer of papier mâché and then leave it to dry.

7

When the papier mâché covering the balloon is dry, pop the balloon and remove it.

Form the ladybug's body by cutting the balloon-shaped papier mâché in half.

8

Take the remaining half of the balloon shape and cut a section from its narrow end.

To form the ladybug's head, bend this slightly and tape it to the narrow end of the body.
Cover the tape with a layer of papier mâché.

9

When all the parts have dried, stick them together, using either double-sided tape or glue.

Cover all the areas where parts join with a layer of papier mâché to strengthen the whole model. Finish your ladybug model by painting in the details.

WARNING! ➡ **Keep wallpaper glue paste away from your mouth and wash hands well after use.**

Rocketeer

ADULT HELP NEEDED!

You will need:

- Scissors, pencil and ruler
- Thin plastic bag
- 3 ft of string
- Sticky tape
- Nose cone and rocket fins (see templates on pages 50-51)
- Needle valve
- Cork
- Thick card
- Large, empty plastic bottle
- Water
- Sticky putty
- Bicycle pump and adapter
- Poster paints

This water-powered rocket will amaze you—it goes very high, very fast! Once it is in the air, watch the parachute and nose cone float safely down to Earth.

1 Start by making the parachute. Cut a 12 in. circle from the plastic bag. Cut four lengths of string, each 9 in. long.

Tape one piece of string to each quarter of the circle, as shown.

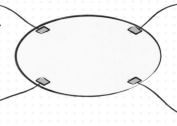

2 Make up and decorate the nose cone (see page 50). Tape one free end of string to each quarter of the nose-cone base. Fold the parachute carefully, as shown. Push the string into the cone, followed by the folded parachute. This should fit loosely in the cone, so it will fall out easily after launch.

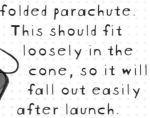

Push the needle valve all the way through the center of the cork.

Ask an adult to help you with this.

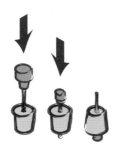 Cut four rocket fins from thick card, following the template on page 51. Decorate the fins, using the poster paints, and stick them to the bottle.

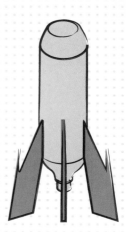

 Quarter fill the bottle with water, then push the cork and needle valve into the mouth of the bottle. If the cork doesn't fit perfectly, use sticky putty to make a tight seal. Take the bottle, nose cone and pump to an open space, such as a park or backyard.

 Turn the bottle upside down and balance it on its fins. Place the nose cone on top of the bottle. Attach the pump to the needle valve and start pumping.

Valve

Cork

Bicycle pump
(with adapter)

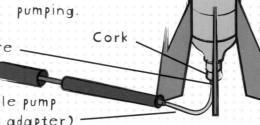

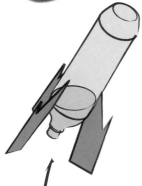 Keep pumping, and the pressure will build up inside the bottle, until the cork explodes out of the bottom. The Rocketeer will shoot way up into the air!

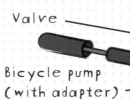

Watch as the nose cone detaches from the rocket, then floats safely back down to Earth.

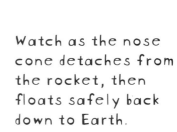

Rocket experiments can be dangerous!
Follow these simple safety rules to avoid accidents!

• **Always launch your rocket in a wide, open space.**
• **Never point the rocket at anyone or anything.**
• **Do not lean over your rocket while you are trying to launch it.**

WARNING!

ROCKETEER TEMPLATES

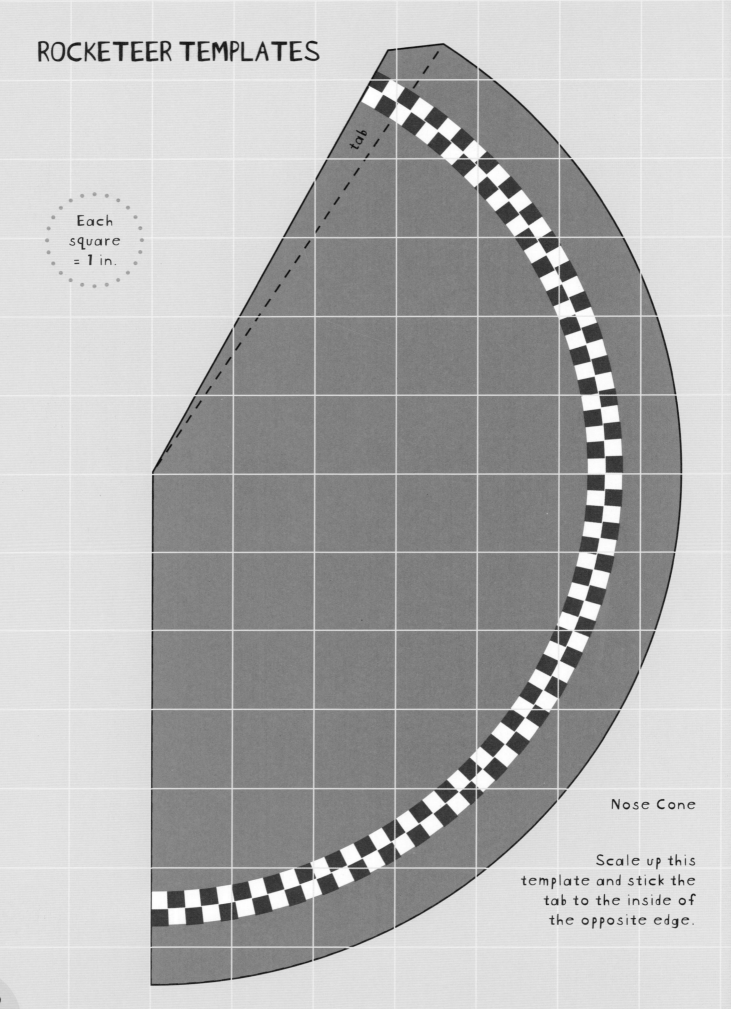

Each square = 1 in.

tab

Nose Cone

Scale up this template and stick the tab to the inside of the opposite edge.

SCALING UP

Throughout this book the term "scale up" is referred to when you need to draw up the templates. This just means drawn up bigger than they appear on the page.

All the squares on these templates are equal to a 1 in. measurement, although they appear smaller. So you need to draw up a grid of squares that measure 1 in. on all sides, onto a piece of thick card. Then, using a pencil and ruler, carefully copy what you see on the template into each square of your grid.

FOLD LINES

- - - - - - - - - - - - - - -

These are fold lines.

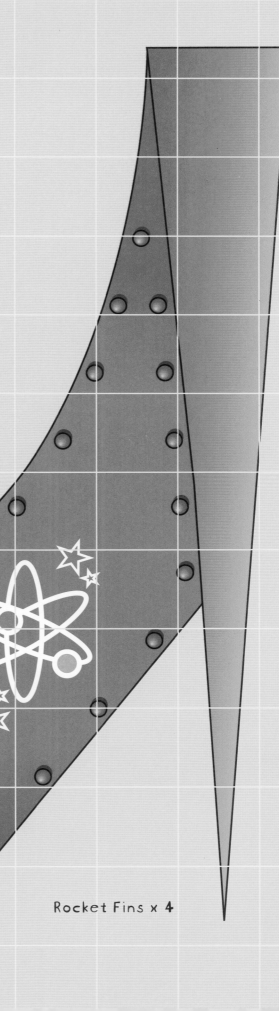

Don't forget to decorate both sides of each fin.

Rocket Fins x 4

Crazy Cookies

You will need:

- 1 stick of butter
- ½ cup superfine sugar
- 1 egg
- 1⅔ cups all-purpose flour
- Baking parchment
- Large bowl
- Wooden spoon
- Sieve
- Rolling pin
- Cookie cutters
- Palette knife
- Cooling rack
- Small bowls
- Icing syringe

ADULT HELP NEEDED!

Let your imagination run wild when decorating these crazy cookies, but watch out that you don't make them look too good to eat!

1 Preheat the oven to 350°F. Grease the baking parchment with a little butter.

Put the butter into the bowl, add the sugar and mix well with the wooden spoon until light and fluffy.

2 Add the egg, mixing in well with the spoon.

Pour flour into the sieve over the bowl and sift into the mixture. Gently mix in the flour.

Using your hands, knead the mixture into a smooth dough. Put into the refrigerator for 15 minutes.

Put the dough onto a floured surface, sprinkle a little flour onto the rolling pin, and roll out the dough, but not too thin. Use the cutters to cut out the cookies and put onto the baking tray using the palette knife.

Bake in the oven for 10 minutes until golden brown. Lift onto the cooling rack to cool before decorating.

Water frosting

- 1 cup confectioner's sugar
- 1-2 tablespoons water
- Food coloring (optional)
- ½ tsp. baking cocoa powder (optional)

Sift the confectioner's sugar into a bowl and add enough water to make a thick smooth paste, using a wooden spoon. Add one or two drops of food coloring. To make chocolate frosting, add ½ tsp. of baking cocoa powder to the confectioner's sugar before sifting.

Royal frosting

- 1 egg white
- 1 cup confectioner's sugar
- Food coloring (optional)

Put an egg white into a small bowl and beat lightly with a fork. Sift the confectioner's sugar into another bowl, add the egg white and beat well until the frosting thickens. Add a drop of food coloring if you wish, to make the frosting a color of your choice.

Pinhole Viewer

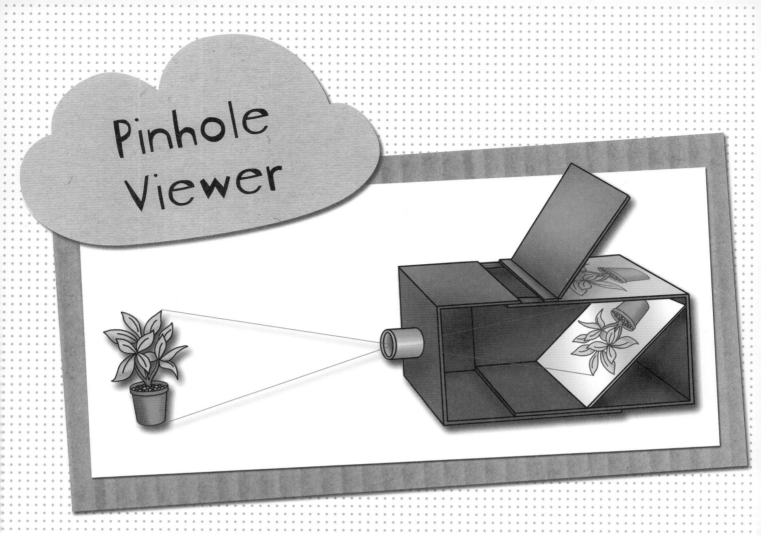

- Shoebox with a lid
- Scissors
- Paintbrush
- Black paint
- Sticky tape
- Piece of tracing paper
- Push pin

A camera obscura projects an image without using a lens. (A pinhole viewer will do the same thing.) Most people believe that the camera obscura was first used to observe the Sun and solar eclipses.

It began to be used by Renaissance artists, like Leonardo da Vinci, to help them understand light patterns. The camera obscura works in a dark room. Images from outside the room appear upside down on the other side of the hole. Make a pinhole viewer to see this in action.

 Cut out one of the small rectangular sides of the shoebox, leaving 1 in. around the edge. Paint the inside of the box black. Tightly tape the lid to the box, making sure no light can get in.

 Cut a piece of tracing paper about ½ in. larger, all the way around, than the cut-out rectangle, and tape it over the hole in the side of the box. This is what you'll look at.

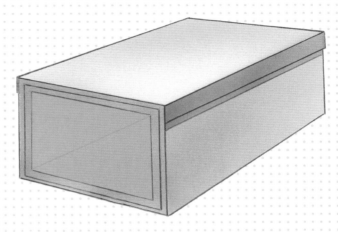

 Make a tiny hole with the push pin in the middle of the end opposite your tracing paper. The smaller the hole, the more sharply focused the image will appear.

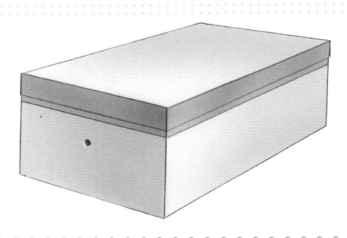

 Stand indoors and point the hole toward the window.

Make sure there's no bright light behind you. You should be able to see the image of the window upside down.

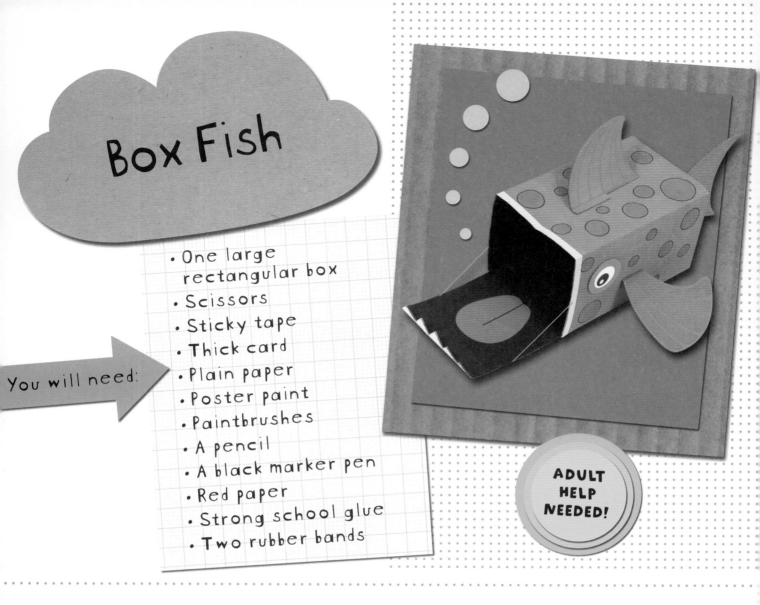

Box Fish

You will need:

- One large rectangular box
- Scissors
- Sticky tape
- **Thick card**
- Plain paper
- Poster paint
- Paintbrushes
- A pencil
- A black marker pen
- Red paper
- Strong school glue
- **Two rubber bands**

ADULT HELP NEEDED!

With its snapping jaws and huge black mouth, this cardboard box fish makes a real splash. Its big eyes keep a lookout for any unsuspecting prey that swims too close, while those sharp-toothed jaws wait to gobble up your dirty laundry. Decorate the model in your favorite colors.

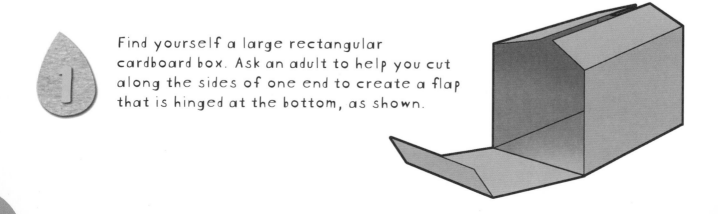

1 Find yourself a large rectangular cardboard box. Ask an adult to help you cut along the sides of one end to create a flap that is hinged at the bottom, as shown.

Use sticky tape to secure the other box flaps shut firmly.

Scale up and copy the tooth template (see page 58) onto card. Use this to draw a row of teeth onto the flap you created in step 1, then cut out the teeth, as shown.

If the cardboard box you have found has printing all over it, cover it up by gluing sheets of plain paper over the outside of the box (including the teeth).

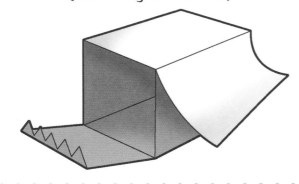

Paint the inside of the box black and the outside orange. When the paint is dry, take a pencil and draw circles of different sizes all over the box. Paint the circles purple. When they are dry, draw an outline around them all with a black marker pen.

Scale up and copy the two eye circle templates (see page 59). Draw the larger one onto a thick sheet of card twice, and the smaller one onto a piece of white paper twice. Cut them out. Paint the card circles a light purple. Draw eye details onto the smaller paper circles with a black marker pen. Glue the white paper circles onto the larger card circles. Now glue the card circles onto either side of the box. Scale up and copy the tongue template (see page 58) onto red paper. Cut this out, and add details with a black marker pen. Stick the tongue to the hinged flap you made in step 1.

Scale up and copy the side fin (two), top fin (one) and tail fin (one) templates (see pages 58–59) onto thick card. Cut them out and paint them orange and purple, as shown. Use glue on the tabs of each fin to fix them in place on the cardboard box body.

Paint a pink lip around the mouth of your fish. With a pencil, make four holes in your fish (two in the mouth flap and two in the box sides) and knot rubber bands through them, as shown, to create a snapping mouth.

BOX FISH TEMPLATES

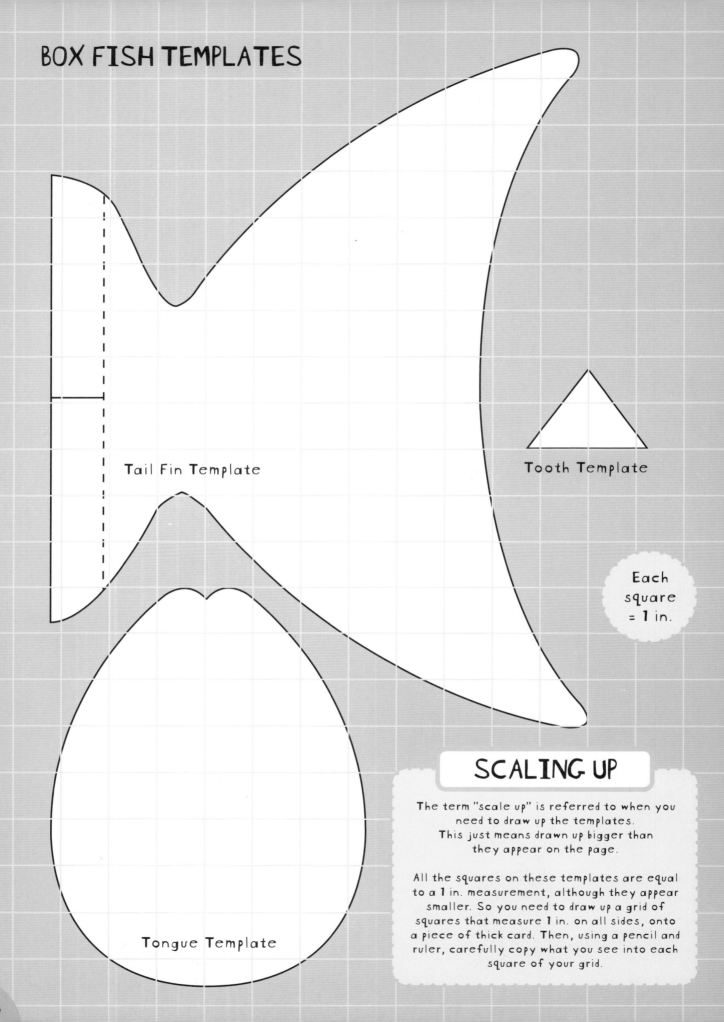

Tail Fin Template

Tooth Template

Tongue Template

Each square = 1 in.

SCALING UP

The term "scale up" is referred to when you need to draw up the templates. This just means drawn up bigger than they appear on the page.

All the squares on these templates are equal to a 1 in. measurement, although they appear smaller. So you need to draw up a grid of squares that measure 1 in. on all sides, onto a piece of thick card. Then, using a pencil and ruler, carefully copy what you see into each square of your grid.

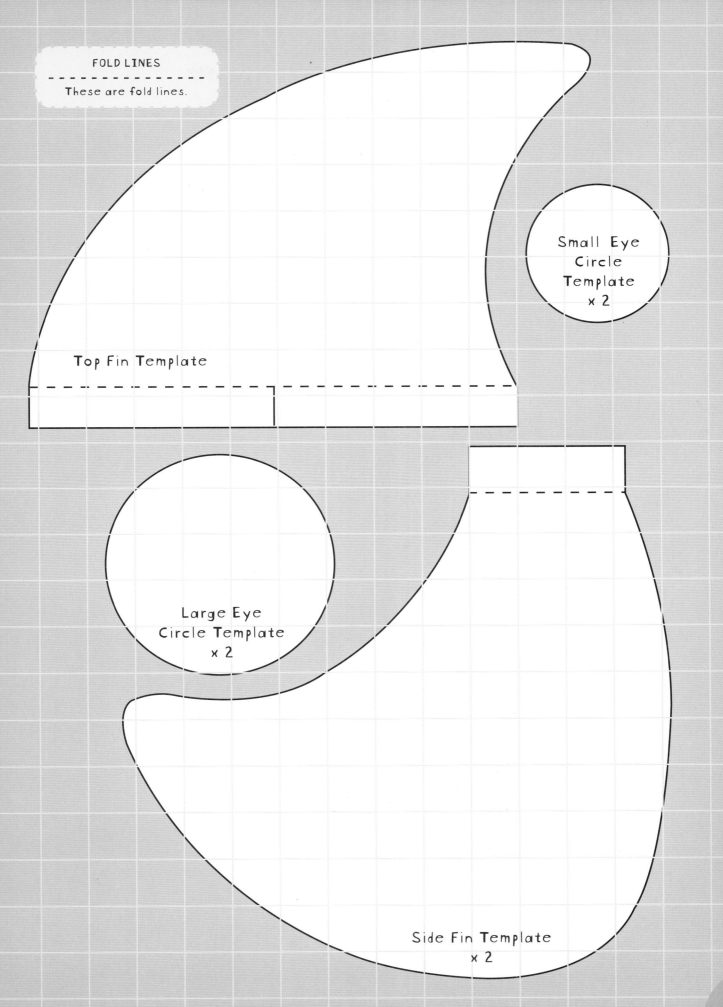

FOLD LINES
- - - - - - - - - - - - -
These are fold lines.

Top Fin Template

Small Eye
Circle
Template
x 2

Large Eye
Circle Template
x 2

Side Fin Template
x 2

Mini Kite

Sail

Rudder

You will nee

- Blue, green and orange tissue (art) paper
- Pencil and ruler
- Scissors
- Two art straws
- Art tape
- Double-sided tape
- 30 ft of thread

This miniature kite is easy to make and can be flown in all wind strengths. Kites like this have been flown since the 17th century.

MINI KITE TEMPLATES

Tails

 **1** To make the kite's sail, copy the sail template onto orange tissue paper. Carefully cut it out with your scissors.

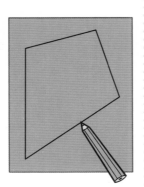

 **2** Cut one straw to 6¾ in. and the other to 4¾ in. in length. These are the kite's spars.

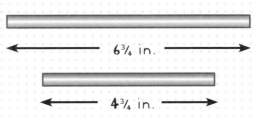

6¾ in.

4¾ in.

 3 Take the long spar and make a pencil mark 2 in. from one end. On the shorter spar, make a mark halfway along.

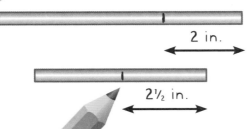

2 in.

2½ in.

 4 Next, hold the spars so that the two pencil marks line up together.

Take a 6 in. strip of art tape and tape the two spars together, as shown.

 5 Stick a thin strip of double-sided tape along the length of both spars. With the long vertical spar facing the sail, carefully stick the spars onto the tissue sail, as shown.

 6 Copy the kite rudder shape onto blue tissue paper and cut it out. Turn the kite over and stick the triangle to the kite with a thin piece of double-sided tape, as shown, about 1 in. from the top.

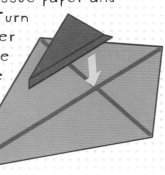

7 Copy the kite tails shape onto the green tissue paper and one from the blue too. Fasten them together at one end with double-sided tape. Using another piece of tape, attach the joined end to the base of the long spar.

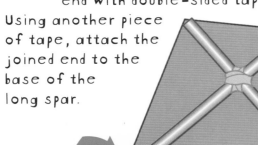

8 Finally, attach one end of the thread to the kite rudder using a small strip of blue tissue paper covered with double-sided tape.

Now you're ready to fly!

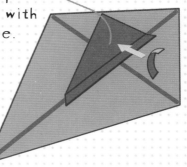

Cool Cupcakes

You will need:

- 1 stick of butter
- 1 cup all-purpose flour
- 2 tsp. baking powder
- 1 cup confectioner's sugar
- 2 eggs
- 2-3 tbsp. full fat milk
- Fresh whipped cream
- Shredded dried colored coconut
- Cupcake tin
- Cupcake liners
- Mixing bowl • Sieve
- Wooden spoon
- Cooling rack

Share these cupcakes with the people that you love. They make great gifts or just have fun baking them and enjoy them yourself!

 1 Put cupcake liners in the cupcake tin. Preheat the oven to 390°F.

 **2** Put the butter into a bowl then sift the flour and baking powder over the top.

3 Use the tips of your fingers to rub the butter and flour and baking powder together until the mixture becomes crumbly.

4 Add the sugar and stir in the eggs. Finally, add enough milk to make the mixture creamy.

5 Put spoonfuls of the mixture into the cupcake liners.

6 Bake the cupcakes for **10–15** minutes, then leave them to cool on a wire rack.

7 Decorate them with a generous swirl of fresh whipped cream. Cover with dried coconut to finish your cool cupcakes.

Fuzzy Flower

- Fuzzy sticks
  (two pink,
  one green,
  half orange)
- Scissors

Set your fingers whizzing to create this pretty flower.
You can buy fuzzy sticks from most craft or hobby shops.
Why not try making lots of different-colored flowers?

 Make a loop at one end of
a pink stick and fold
over the tip, as
shown.

 Make a second loop and twist
the remaining stick
around the tip.

 Make a third petal, twist the
stick around the tip again and
leave a stump.

Make another set of petals using the second pink stick, then join the two sets of petals together by twisting the stumps.

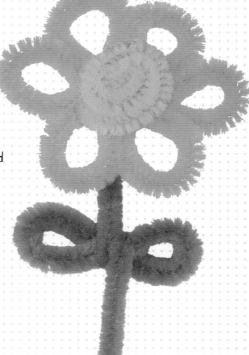

Make a swirl with the orange stick, leaving a 1 in. stump at the end.

Join the swirl to the petals by folding the 1 in. stump around the back of the petals.

Take the green fuzzy stick and cut it in half.

Bend the stump of the orange swirl over to hold the green stem in place.

Make a "figure eight" with the remaining green stick and twist the ends together.

Wrap the stem around the center of the leaves to hold them in place to finish.

Friendship Bracelet

You will need:

- String
- Scissors
- Clipboard
- Thin yarn threads in four colors (two threads of each color, 1 yard long)

One of the best things about making friendship bracelets is that you don't need many tools or materials. This fantastic bracelet is a great project to get you started! Before you begin, go online to learn how to make left-loop full knots and right-loop full knots, as you'll need these.

1 Wrap a piece of string around the wrist of the person you are making the bracelet for. Cut the string so you know how long the bracelet needs to be.

2 Cut the threads you need to the right length and knot them together, leaving about 2 in. of loose thread at the end. Clip them to your weaving card (a clipboard, or a piece of cardboard with a clip at the top).

3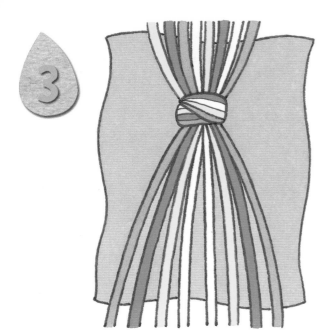

Knot the eight threads together at the top (we have used orange, red, yellow and white). On the weaving card, position the two white threads in the middle. Then place the other threads on either side of the central threads so that the colors mirror each other (orange on the outside, then red, then yellow).

4 Use the left-hand thread to make left-loop full knots over the three threads next to it, and leave it in the middle.

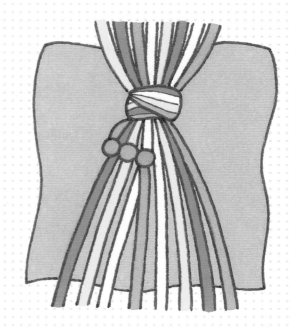

5 Use the right-hand threads to make right-loop full knots into the middle. Knot the two orange threads together.

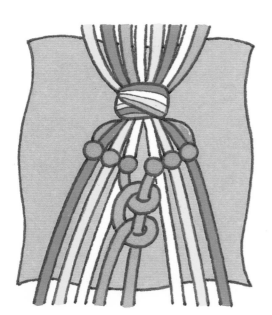

6 Continue knotting from left to center then right to center, and knotting in the middle, to make three more rows. The threads will now be back in the same order that you started with.

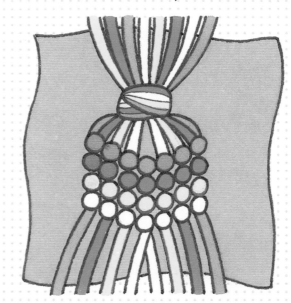

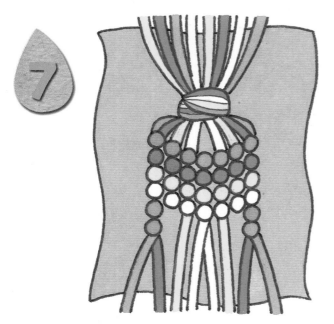

Use the left-hand thread to make two left-loop full knots over the next thread. Leave the left-hand thread on the outside. Use the right-hand thread to make two right-loop full knots over the next threads. Leave the right-hand thread on the outside.

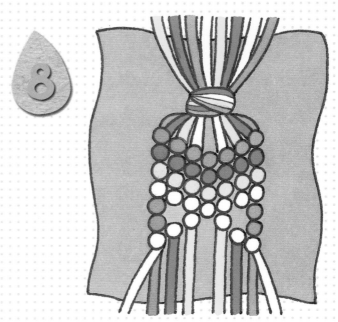

Move to the middle threads. Knot the right-middle thread over all the threads to the right using left-loop full knots. Knot the left-middle thread over all the threads to the left using right-loop full knots.

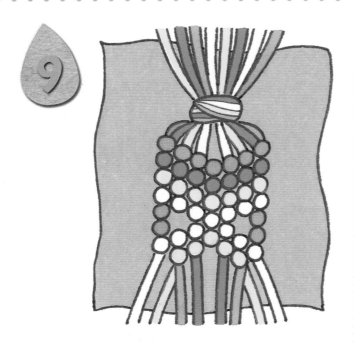

Knot the new middle threads together. Knot the right-middle thread over the next thread and the one after that, using left-loop full knots. Knot the left-middle thread over the next thread and the one after that, using right-loop full knots.

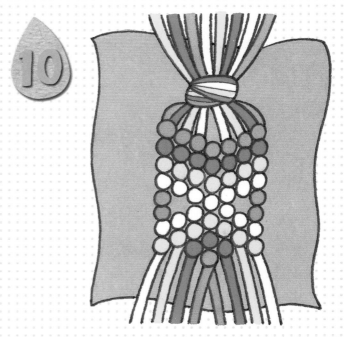

Knot the new middle threads together. Knot the right-middle thread over the next thread, using a left-loop full knot. Knot the left-middle thread over the next thread, using a right-loop full knot. Knot the new middle threads together.

11 Use the thread on the left of the middle threads to make a left-loop full knot over the left-middle thread next to it.

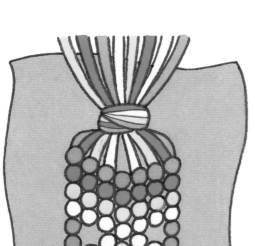

Use the thread on the right of the middle threads to make a right-loop full knot over the right-middle thread next to it. Knot the new middle threads together.

12 In the same way as in step **11**, knot the threads third from the middle into the center and knot them together.

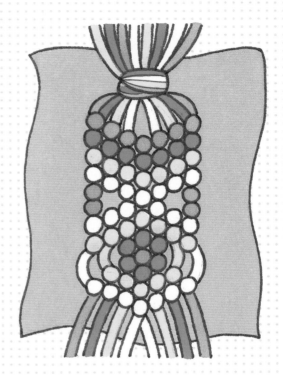

Then knot the outside threads into the middle and knot them together. The threads will now be in the order that you started with.

13 Keep following steps **4** to **12** until the bracelet is the same length as your measuring string.

14 Tie a knot to finish off the bracelet, and trim off any loose thread about 1¾ in. from the knot.

Coin Vanish

You will need:
- A coin
- Magic wand (or pencil)

This illusion is useful to know for other tricks where you have to make a coin or small object disappear.

1 Hold a coin by its edge as in the picture.

Keep your free fingers out of the way so the coin can be seen clearly.

2 Place the coin against the open palm of your left hand and close your left fingers over it.

3

Keep hold of the coin with your right hand, but allow your fingers to relax until they rest on the back of the fingers of your left hand.

4 Now move your left hand away with your fingers hiding the coin. Reach into your pocket with your right hand, and bring out your magic wand.

5

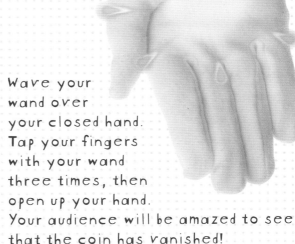

Wave your wand over your closed hand. Tap your fingers with your wand three times, then open up your hand. Your audience will be amazed to see that the coin has vanished!

But how?

The coin never actually moves into your left hand, although it should look as if it does. Really, the coin stays in your right hand and you drop it into your pocket as you produce your wand. Watch your left hand all the time, and try to forget about your right, and your audience will follow your gaze.

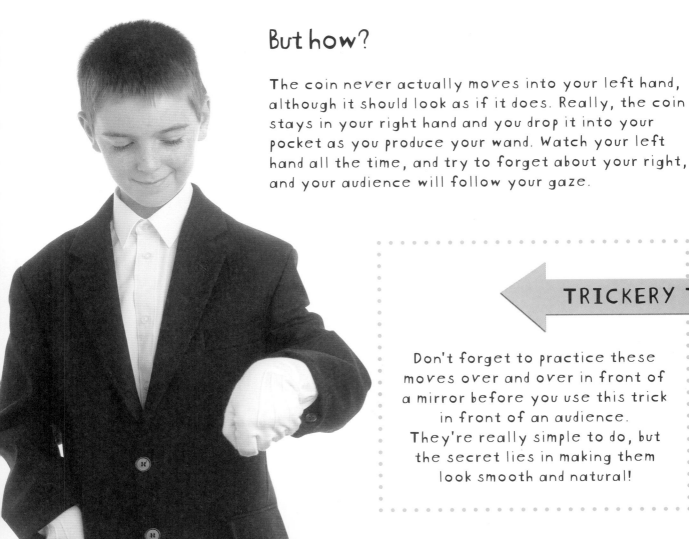

TRICKERY TIP

Don't forget to practice these moves over and over in front of a mirror before you use this trick in front of an audience. They're really simple to do, but the secret lies in making them look smooth and natural!

Balloon Dog

You will need:
- One long balloon
- A black marker pen (optional)

Balloon animals are fun! Make this dog with just one long balloon!

 **1** Inflate the balloon to 24 in. in length.

 **2** Twist two 3½ in. bubbles at the knotted end of the balloon. Fold the second bubble over and twist it around the first bubble to make a nose and ears.

 **3**

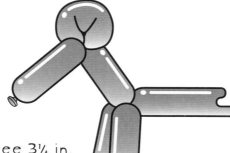

Make three 3¼ in. bubbles along the balloon. Twist the first and third bubbles together to make a neck and two front legs.

 **4** Make three more bubbles: 4 in. and two 3¼ in. Twist the first and third bubbles together for a body and back legs.

Turn the back legs so that they line up with the front ones.

 5 The remaining part of the balloon will form your balloon dog's tail. Draw eyes and a mouth with a black marker pen.

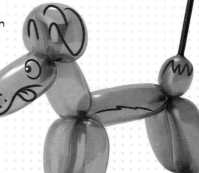

Papier Mâché Letters

ADULT HELP NEEDED!

You will need:

- Bowl
- Wallpaper glue paste
- Spoon
- Newspaper
- Card or old cloth
- Paintbrush and paints
- Re-sealable container

Let your imagination run wild with these papier mâché letters! If you have any papier mâché mix left, put it in the re-sealable container to use again. It should last for three to four days.

1 Ask an adult to make up the wallpaper glue paste with water following the pack instructions.

2 Tear up lots of small strips of old newspaper and stir them into the paste.

Keep adding newspaper strips until your mixture is thick.

3 Cover your work surface with a piece of card or old cloth. Then, using small lumps of papier mâché, layer and shape your letters. Leave the letters to dry overnight.

4 When your letters are completely dry, they are ready to be decorated. Paint them in bright colors, cover them in spots or get creative with lines and swirls. Once the letters have dried, you can use them to make posters, greeting cards or a name plaque for your room.

Keep wallpaper paste away from your mouth and wash hands well after use.

WARNING!

73

Funny Skittles

- Balloon
- Newspaper
- Wallpaper glue paste
- String
- Paint and paintbrushes
- Six small soda bottles and lids
- Colored card
- Scissors
- White paper
- A black marker pen
- Strong school glue

ADULT HELP NEEDED!

Make this fantastic game and you can challenge your friends to see who can get the highest score by knocking over these funny skittles, then stand them back up and try again!

1 Ask an adult to make up the wallpaper glue paste with water following the pack instructions.

2 Inflate a balloon so that it is approx 4 in. across and round in shape. Tear a newspaper into small squares, roughly 1 in. x 1 in., and use wallpaper glue paste to cover the balloon with seven layers of papier mâché.

3 Tie a piece of string around the neck of the balloon, as shown, and hang it somewhere warm to dry.

4 Once the papier mâché is dry, pop the balloon and remove it from the ball shape. Paint the ball with a base coat of dark purple. When it has dried, dry brush on a coat of light purple.

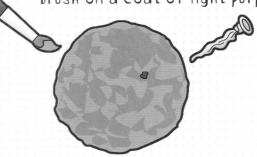

5 Find six clean, small soda bottles with lids. Pour a little paint (any color) into one of the bottles and tightly screw on the lid. Shake the bottle until the paint completely covers the inside of it. Then, into two of the bottles pour some more paint of a different color, and shake them. Repeat the action, using a different color, for the last three bottles.

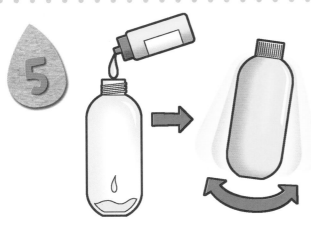

6 Copy the cute character pictures opposite onto card. Cut them out, then decorate each of your cute characters in a different way, giving them different facial expressions.

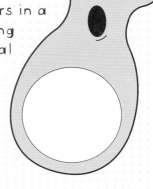

7 Use glue to fix each cardboard character onto one of the colored bottles and you're ready to play funny skittles!

WARNING! → **Keep wallpaper paste away from your mouth and wash hands well after use.**

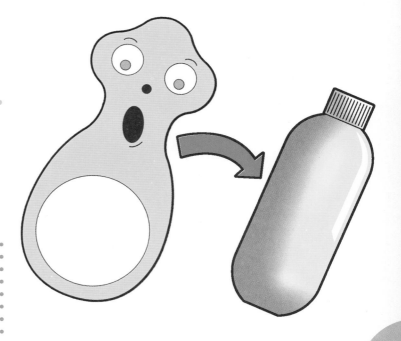

Totem Pole

- Three small round potato chip cartons (two with lids)
- Colored paper (red, yellow, blue)
- Scissors and ruler
- A black marker pen
- Strong school glue
- Thin card
- White paper
- Colored card (green, red, yellow, blue, orange)
- Two pencils

ADULT HELP NEEDED!

It's hard to believe that this awesome totem pole was once three potato chip cartons! Use it to store your favorite pens, pencils, rubbers...whatever you like!

1 Find three small round potato chip cartons: two of them must have their lids. Cover up the printing by sticking a length of colored paper around each one, as shown. (Make one red, one yellow and one blue.)

2 Cut six strips of colored paper that are 1 in. wide and long enough to go around the tubes.

Make two red, two yellow and two blue. Add details to the strips with a black marker pen. Glue the red strips to the yellow carton, the yellow strips to the blue carton, and the blue strips to the red carton.

3 Scale up and copy the eye template (see page 79) onto thin card. Draw around it six times onto a sheet of white paper and cut them all out. Add details to each eye with a black marker pen.

Glue two eyes onto each carton, as shown.

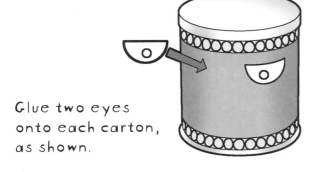

4 Scale up and copy the three nose templates. Draw around each one twice onto green card and then cut them out. Glue each pair together, leaving the tabs free of glue. Now glue the tabs of each nose onto a carton, as shown. Add different cheek and eyebrow details to each face with a black marker pen, as shown.

5 Scale up and copy the straight arm template provided onto red card and cut out two.

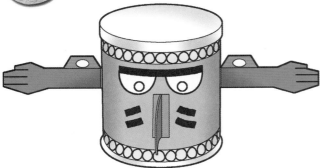

Draw on fingers with a black marker pen and bend the tabs into shape. Use the tabs to glue an arm onto either side of the blue carton, as shown. Push its lid back on.

6 Scale up and copy the bent arm template provided onto yellow card and cut out two.

Draw on fingers with a black marker pen and bend the tabs into shape. Use the tabs to glue an arm onto either side of the red carton, as shown. Push its lid back on.

7 Scale up and copy the ear template provided onto blue card and cut out two. Draw on details with a black marker pen and bend the tabs into shape. Use the tabs to glue an ear onto either side of the yellow carton, as shown.

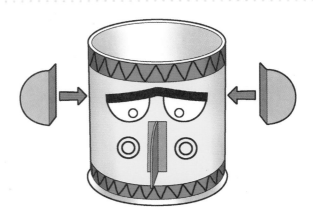

Scale up and copy the feather and circle templates provided. Draw two feathers onto orange card and one onto red card and cut them out. Draw one circle onto green card and cut this out.

Glue all these together, as shown, and add details with a black marker pen.

Glue the feather headdress made in step 8 onto the top of the yellow carton, as shown.

Scale up and copy the feet template provided onto orange card. Cut this out and add details with a black marker pen, as shown.

Glue the feet onto the base of the red carton, as shown.

Place the cartons on top of one another, as shown. Ask an adult to help you cut out the holes marked in the arms and store your pencils here. You could keep your pens at the top and store your erasers, sharpeners and keepsakes in the bottom two heads.

TOTEM POLE TEMPLATES

SCALING UP

The term "scale up" is referred to when you need to draw up the templates. This just means drawn up bigger than they appear on the page.

All the squares on these templates are equal to a 1 in. measurement, although they appear smaller. So you need to draw up a grid of squares that measure 1 in. on all sides, onto a piece of thick card. Then, using a pencil and ruler, carefully copy what you see into each square of your grid.

Each square = 1 in.

FOLD LINES
- - - - - - - -
These are fold lines.

Feather Template x 3

Feet Template

Straight Arm Template x 2

x 2   x 2   x 2

Nose Templates

Bent Arm Template x 2

Ear Template x 2

Circle Template

Eye Template x 6

Radical Racer

ADULT HELP NEEDED!

You will need:

- Three fabric softener bottles
- Scissors, pencil and ruler
- Thick card
- A cardboard box approx 7 in. x 5 in. x 2 in.
- An egg carton
- Strong school glue
- Art tape
- Four large round potato chip cartons
- Corrugated card
- Two bottle lids
- A large cardboard poster tube
- Paint and paintbrushes
- A black marker pen
- Good quality white paper
- Yellow paper
- Thin white card

Race into tomorrow with this futuristic car! This is one mean machine, snarling at the starting line, waiting for the green light to go, go, go... With a set of huge wheels, chunky tires and state-of-the-art spoiler, this radical racer is sure to make heads turn!

Begin by finding two fabric softener bottles.

Carefully cut away one side of each, as shown. (Ask an adult to do this for you.)

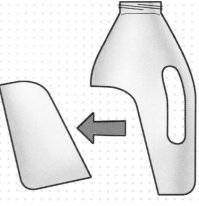

Scale up and copy the thruster support template (see page 86) onto a sheet of thick card and cut it out.

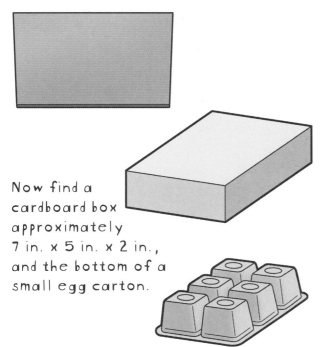

Now find a cardboard box approximately 7 in. x 5 in. x 2 in., and the bottom of a small egg carton.

Using glue and plenty of art tape, fix the cardboard box and the egg carton onto either side of the thruster support (make sure they are in the center).

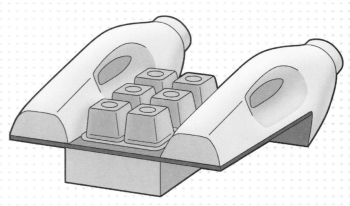

Now fix the two fabric softener bottles onto the ends of the thruster support so that they sit either side of the egg carton, as shown.

Scale up and copy the rear spoiler (x 2) and the rear spoiler support (x 2) templates (see page 86) onto a sheet of thick card and cut out.

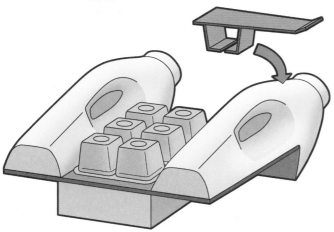

Using art tape and glue, fix these onto the top of the fabric softener bottles, as shown.

Find four large potato chip cartons. Cut each of these down so that they are all 3 in. (approx) in height.

Glue a disk of thick card into the open end of each carton to give you a basic wheel shape.

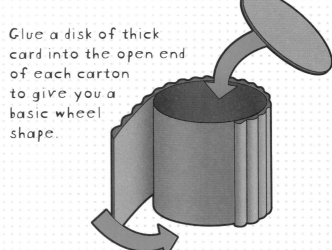

Cover the outside of each carton with a strip of corrugated card to create tires.

6 Carefully glue the wheels from step 5 onto either side of the cardboard box from step 3. Find two bottle lids. Glue these onto the cardboard box, as shown, to complete the rear half of the car.

7 Take another fabric softener bottle. Carefully cut away the shape shown (ask an adult to do this for you).

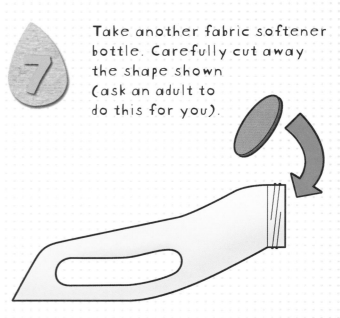

Glue a disk of thick card into the neck of the bottle to seal it off.

8 Find a large cardboard poster tube. Cut four segments from it that all measure 2 in. in length. Glue a disk of thick card into the open ends of each segment, to give a basic wheel shape.

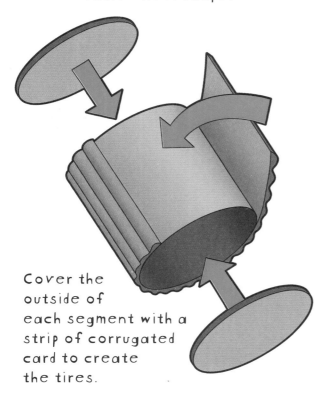

Cover the outside of each segment with a strip of corrugated card to create the tires.

9 Scale up and copy the front wheel support, front spoiler and body templates (see pages 85–87) onto a sheet of thick card, and cut these out.

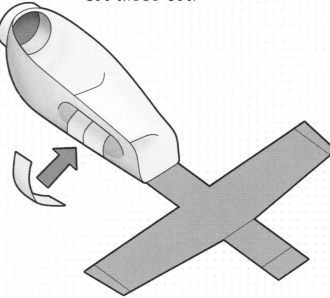

Using glue and art tape, fix the front spoiler onto the fabric softener bottle from step 7, as shown. Fasten it securely by sticking strips of art tape around the sides of the bottle.

Use more glue and strips of art tape to fix the body onto the fabric softener bottle.

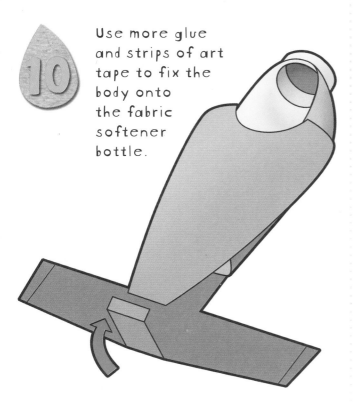

Bend the tab at the front of the spoiler and glue it onto the body, as shown.

Glue and tape the front wheel support onto the fabric softener bottle and body, as shown.

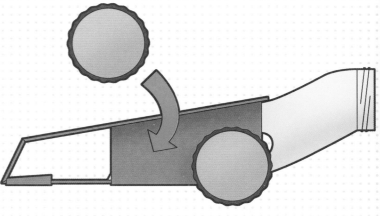

Now glue the wheels from step 8 onto either side of the front wheel support to complete the front end of the car.

Scale up and copy the front/rear support (see page 87) onto a sheet of thick card and cut it out. Glue this beneath the racer to keep the two halves together, as shown. Make sure that you glue the disk of card in the neck of the fabric softener bottle onto the cardboard box on the rear of the car for extra strength.

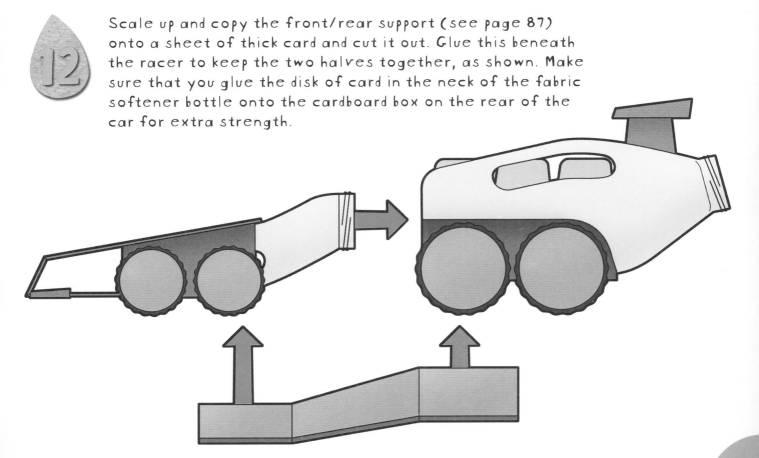

Paint the model a combination of blue, red and gray, as shown.

Add black racing stripes with a marker pen and disks of good quality white paper to the front and sides of the car, and paint a racing number onto these.

Cut out four disks of yellow paper to fit the rear wheels and four disks to fit the front wheels. Draw a wheel design onto each of these disks (make sure they all look the same!). Carefully glue each of these onto the correct size wheels.

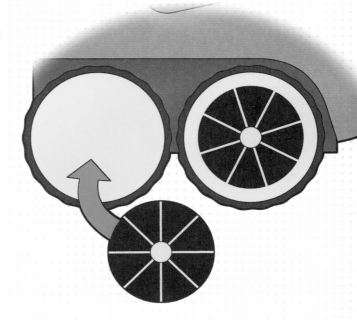

Add the cockpit details by making a windshield from thin white card. Add a steering wheel made from thick card and a seat made from corrugated card, as shown.

RADICAL RACER TEMPLATES

SCALING UP

The term "scale up" is referred to when you need to draw up the templates. This just means drawn up bigger than they appear on the page.

All the squares on these templates are equal to a 1 in. measurement, although they appear smaller. So you need to draw up a grid of squares that measure 1 in. on all sides, onto a piece of thick card. Then, using a pencil and ruler, carefully copy what you see into each square of your grid.

Each square = 1 in.

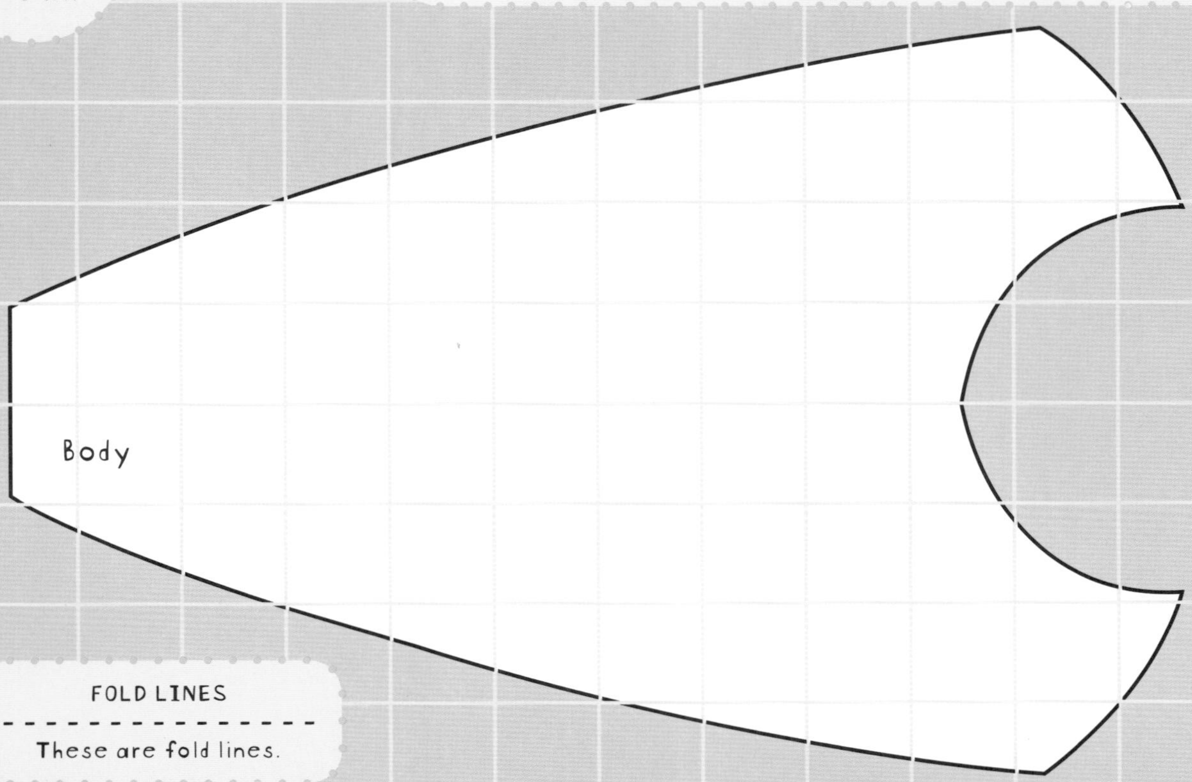

Body

FOLD LINES
- - - - - - - - -
These are fold lines.

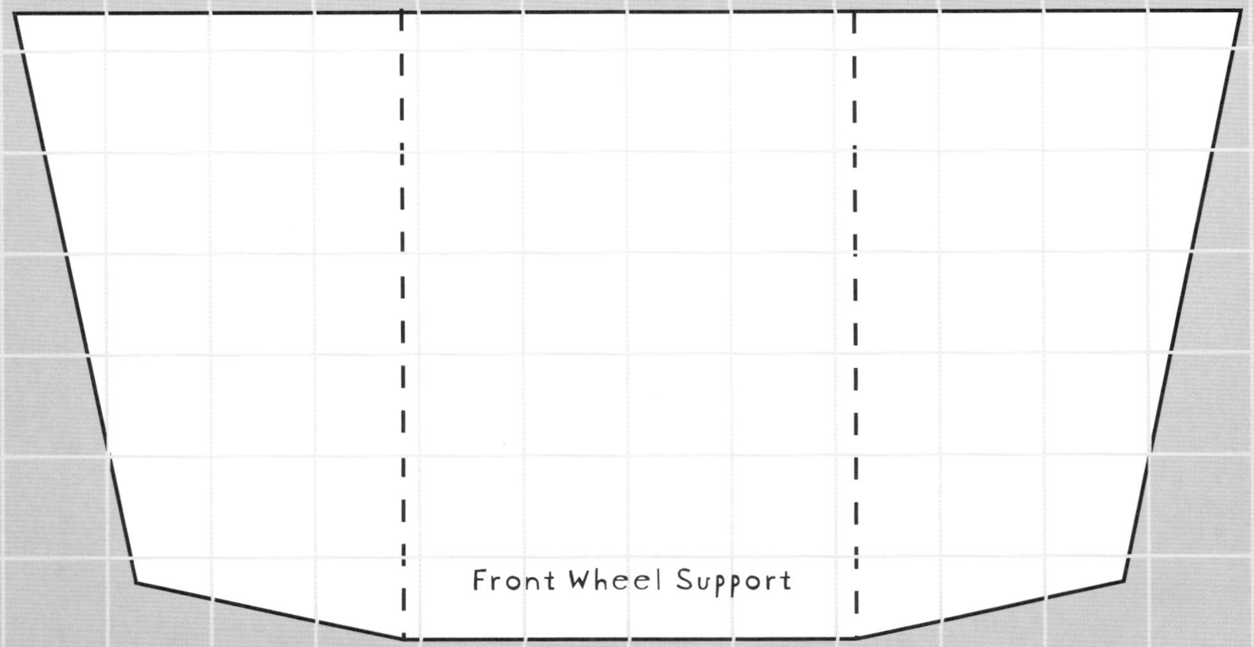

Front Wheel Support

RADICAL RACER TEMPLATES

Each square = 1 in.

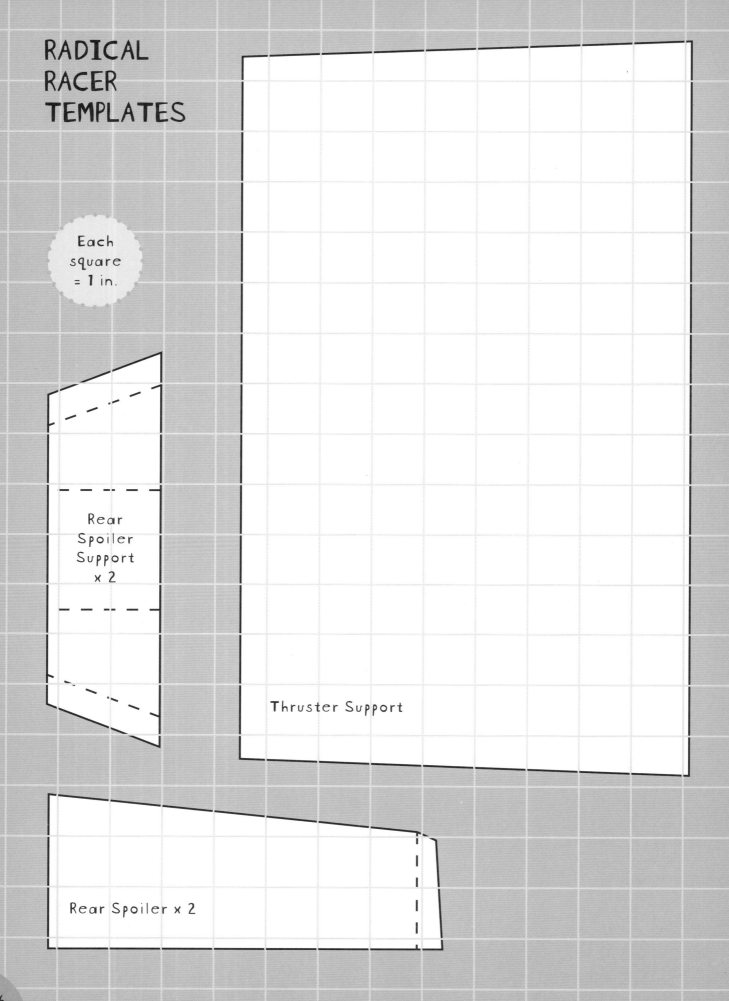

Rear Spoiler Support x 2

Thruster Support

Rear Spoiler x 2

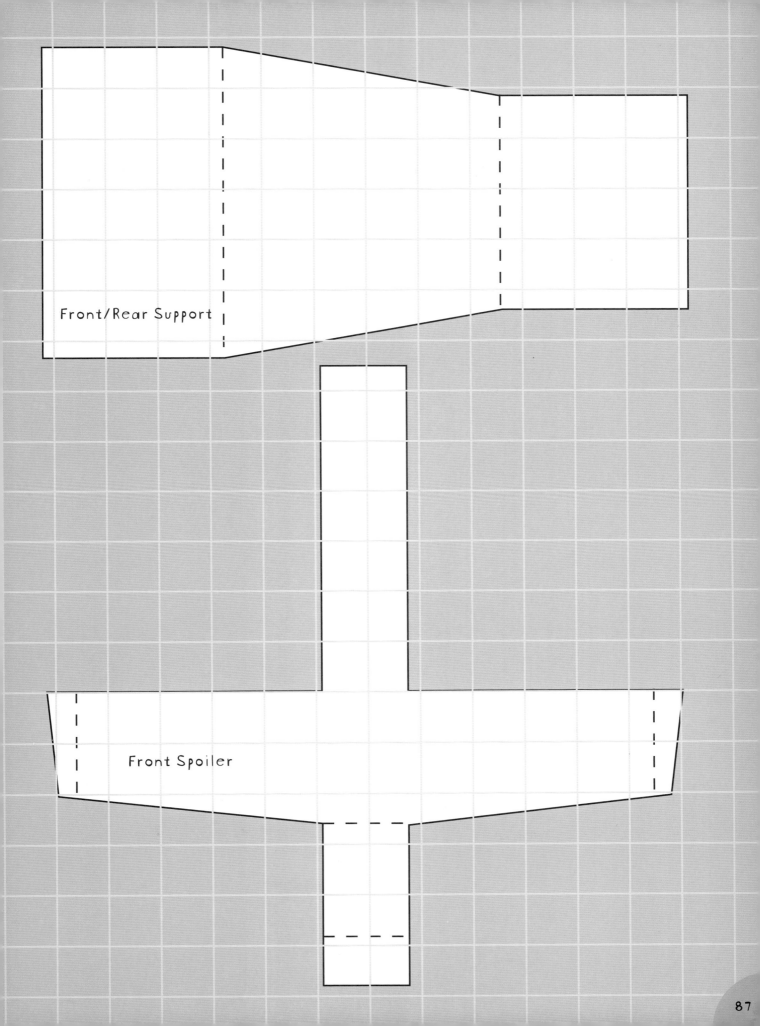

Front/Rear Support

Front Spoiler

Blueberry Muffins

You will need:

- ½ stick of butter
- 2 eggs
- 1 cup sugar
- 2 cups all-purpose flour
- 2 tsp. baking powder
- 7 tbsp. milk
- A dash of vanilla essence
- 1½ cups blueberries
- A muffin baking tray
- Paper cases
- Mixing bowl
- Fork
- Sieve
- Wooden spoon
- Teaspoon

ADULT HELP NEEDED!

These mouth-watering muffins are packed with blueberries!

 Place the paper cases in the muffin tray. Preheat the oven to 350°F.

2 Add the butter, eggs and sugar to a large bowl. Beat them until well mixed.

Mix the flour with the baking powder and sift into the first mixture, alternating with the milk.

4 Blend in the vanilla essence and add the blueberries. Mix everything together until just moistened.

5 Use a spoon to divide the mixture equally into the muffin tray.

Bake the muffins for 30 minutes or until golden brown.

6 Leave the muffins in the tray until they are cool, and then enjoy!

Steady Hand Game

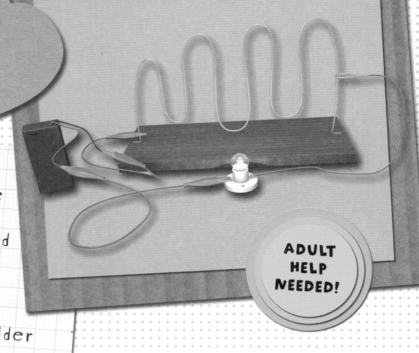

You will need:

- Pair of pliers
- Uncoated wire hanger
- **10 in. insulated copper wire**
- Scissors
- Sticky tape
- Bulb and bulb holder
- Small screwdriver
- **Two electrical lead wires with clips at each end**
- Battery casing and two AA batteries
- Staples
- Hammer
- Block of wood measuring about 20 in. x 10 in.

In the Steady Hand Game, a circuit is made when the wire loop touches the wire hanger—the current flows around the circuit and this is what makes the bulb light up. If you're good at the game, you won't touch the wire, which means the circuit is never completed and the bulb doesn't light up.

1

Use the pliers to cut a 2½ in. length from the wire hanger. Bend it into an open loop, as shown. This is the piece you will hold to test how steady your hand is!

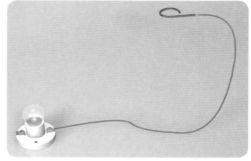

2

Ask an adult to help you strip 1 in. from each end of the insulated copper wire. Wind one end of the wire around the loop made in step 1, securing it with sticky tape if necessary. Attach the other end to the bulb holder—tighten the screw to keep it in place.

Clip a piece of electrical lead wire to one of the battery casing wires, and to the free screw on the bulb holder.

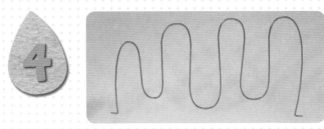

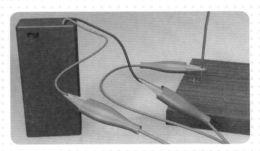

Wrap sticky tape around the ends of the remaining hanger wire. Bend the wire into a wavy shape—make it as complicated as you like.

Hammer the staples over the ends of the wavy wire, securing it to the block of wood.

Clip one end of the remaining electrical lead wire to the wire hanger, and the other end to the free battery casing wire.

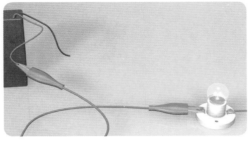

Bend the open loop around one end of the wavy wire, then close up the loop with the pliers.

Unscrew the battery casing and insert the batteries as shown on the diagram inside it. Clip it back together and fasten the screw. Push the switch to the "on" position, and you're ready to play! The aim is to move the wire loop all the way along the wavy wire without touching it.

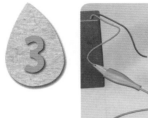

WARNING!

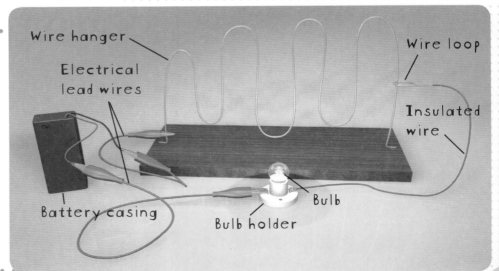

Wire hanger

Electrical lead wires

Wire loop

Insulated wire

Battery casing

Bulb

Bulb holder

Dinosaur Clay Model

You will need:
- Modeling clay (green and white)
- A pencil
- A black marker pen

Arguably the most noisy dinosaur that ever existed, scientists believe that the Parasaurolophus used the long crest on its head to bellow out sound like a musical instrument. Follow these steps to make a dinosaur model out of clay!

Roll a large amount of green modeling clay to make the Parasaurolophus (about the size of a large potato).

For the body, break off roughly half of this amount and shape it into a slightly flattened kidney shape, as shown. Make a large and a small indent on each side of this shape.

To make the tail, roll a medium-sized green carrot shape. Bend the narrow end slightly to form a hook.

For the legs, mold two large cone shapes from green clay.

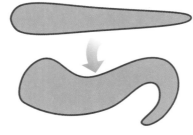

Flatten and round the large end of each and pinch the narrow end to form the toes.

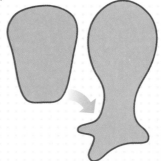

To make the arms, roll two small green carrot shapes.

Flatten and round both ends and bend each arm in the middle.

For the neck, mold a green carrot shape. Flatten both ends on opposite sides and bend into a subtle "S" shape. Avoiding the indents, attach the neck onto the body made in step 2.

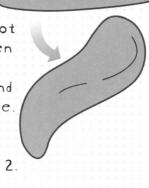

Mold a medium-sized ball of green clay into a wedge shape to form the head. Round off the edges and indent the sides slightly. Flatten the narrow end to look like a duck's bill and add a slit for the mouth. Add two holes for nostrils using a pencil.

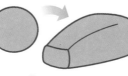

To make the crest, roll a hot dog shape. Pinch one end and flatten the other to form a horn shape.

Make the eyes by molding two small disks of white clay. Stick the eyes and crest onto the head, as shown on the completed model.

Add some white to the green clay to make several lime colored spots. Add them to the body and legs.

Next, roll four small cones of lime green clay. Bend each one in the middle and position two at the end of each arm, as claws.

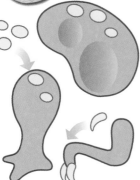

To complete your Parasaurolophus, stick the legs and arms onto the body at the indentation marks made in step 2.

Attach the head and tail onto the body. Use a marker pen to give the Parasaurolophus some pupils.

Shimmering Stars

You will need:

- 5 large popsicle sticks
- Tracing paper
- Pencil
- Strong school glue
- Clothes pegs
- Paint
- Paintbrush
- Colored glitter
- A plastic container or dish
- Ribbon (optional)

These simple shimmering stars look great as Christmas decorations!

1 You need to arrange five popsicle sticks into a star shape. This is quite tricky so trace the template from this page and use this to build your star on. It will help you to get the angles right.

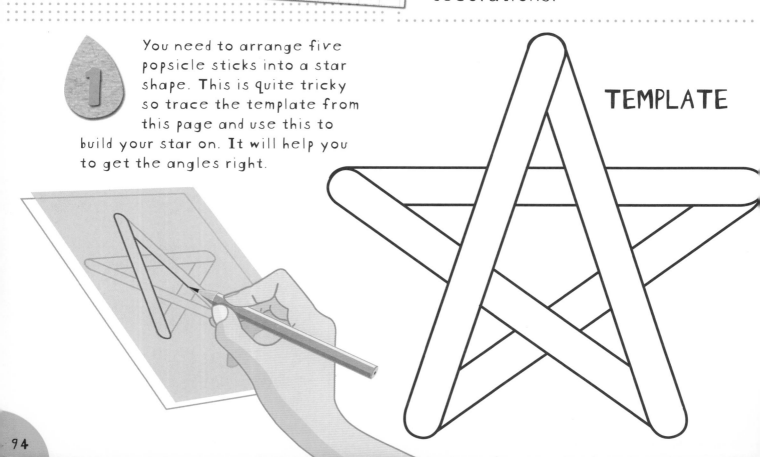

TEMPLATE

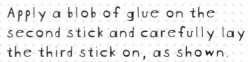

2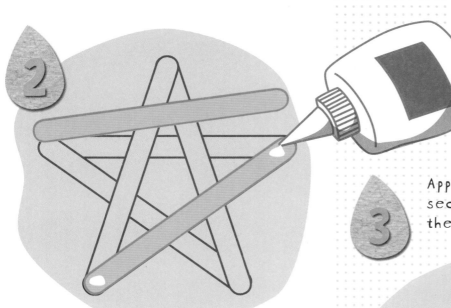

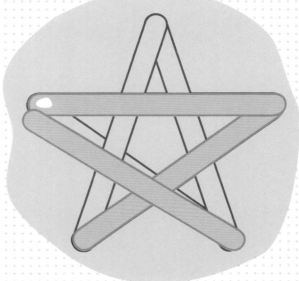

Apply a blob of glue on the second stick and carefully lay the third stick on, as shown.

3

Begin by placing one popsicle stick on the star template, then apply a blob of glue on each end.
Lay the second stick on the template, carefully placing one end over the blob of glue.

4 Now apply a blob of glue on the third stick and carefully lay the fourth stick on.

5 Repeat with the fifth stick. The best way to get your star to stick is to pinch each joint together with a clothes peg, as shown, and allow to dry.

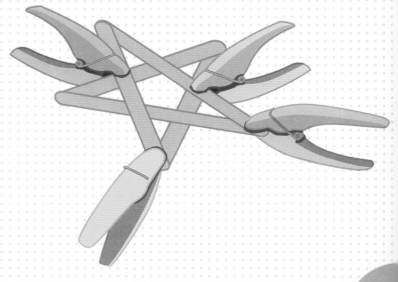

Once the glue is dry, remove the pegs and paint the star a color which will match the glitter you want to use. Allow to dry.

When the paint is dry, coat the star with a thin layer of glue.

Place in a container and carefully sprinkle with glitter, ensuring you cover it completely. Shake the loose glitter off and allow to dry.

When your star is dry it is ready to display. Why not tie a ribbon through one of the points to hang it.